The Watson Guides™

How to Get RICH Selling Cars to *Women!*

Praise for
How to Get RICH Selling Cars to Women

"This is a must read for EVERYONE in the retail automobile business. Women, like just about everyone, wish to be treated with respect. They despise unprofessional behavior and will not tolerate it regardless of price. This book will show you how to earn a woman's trust and respect...and her business."

Michael E. Gorman, *Corporate Director of Training*
GERMAIN MOTOR COMPANY

"I have seen Rebecca transform audiences of automotive sales and service professionals in her interactive seminars. This book is for anyone in our industry willing to learn the competencies needed to harness the economic power of the women's market. They're in the driver's seat now."

John Pockrus, *Area Executive*
AUDI OF AMERICA

"WOW! I've been in the car business for over 20 years, and I've never read a book so knowledgeable on selling to women. It has already increased our sales. Everyone that works for me will get a copy of this book!"

Brad Johnson, *General Manager*
BYERS DUBLIN CHEVROLET

"I have spent most of my 32 year career targeting women auto buyers and now, thanks to Rebecca and Marti, I have a play-book!"

Gabe Staino, *Dealer Principle*
GALLOWAY CHRYSLER, DODGE

"How to Get RICH Selling Cars to Women is destined to become the gold standard for our industry."

Bob Chapman, *Dealer Principle*
BOB CHAPMAN FORD-MERCURY
World's Oldest Ford Dealer

"This book is a great tool for all sales and service personnel. It is easy to understand and, more importantly, easy to implement…a great insight to a misunderstood and lucrative market."
Scott Lustgarten, President
MARTIN DEALERSHIP GROUP
Honda Lexus Dodge Chrysler Plymouth Jeep Subaru Mazda Kia

"I have heard Rebecca's seminar and I am thrilled that she and Marti have taken the time to make their insightful words of wisdom available to all of us, particularly in this unique, fun, and compelling form. Don't miss the opportunity to read this book, written by individuals who have spent the past ten years studying and practicing how to sell to women."
Niki O'Neal, Chief Financial Officer
STUART JEEP, STUART VOLKSWAGEN, STUART MITSUBISHI

"Every salesperson in every dealership will benefit from following the guidelines recommend by Rebecca and Marti in How to Get RICH Selling Cars to Women! Read this book, try the suggestions, and count the number of additional cars you sell each and every month!"
Aaron Masterton, Vice President and General Manager
DENNIS AUTOPOINT
Hyundai Mitsubishi Pontiac Daewoo

"At first, we were skeptical as to what Rebecca's seminar could bring to the table for a veteran group of salespersons and managers. After the seminar, there was no doubt that we were missing opportunities as to how we could better sell sales and service to the female buyer. This book will probably be read by your competitor. Don't take the chance that you may lose even one sale by not reading this book."
Robert A. Layman, Dealer Principle
BOBBY LAYMAN CHEVROLET

The Watson Guides™

How to Get
RICH
Selling Cars
to *Women!*

Rebecca Maddox, M.B.A., C.P.A.
Marti Smye, Ph.D.

with **Denise Ciencin**, M.A.
and *New York Times* bestseller **Scott Ciencin**

MaddoxSmye, LLC
FLORIDA

Published by
MaddoxSmye, LLC
300 Fifth Avenue South, Suite 101
Naples, Florida 34102

Library of Congress Cataloging-in-Publication Data

Maddox, Rebecca; Smye, Marti;
Ciencin, Denise; and Ciencin, Scott.
The Watson Guides: How to Get Rich Selling Cars to
Women / Rebecca Maddox, Marti Smye,
Denise Ciencin, and Scott Ciencin.
p. cm.
ISBN 0-9727637-0-8
Library of Congress Catalog Number 2002096751

Printed in Canada
10 9 8 7 6 5 4 3 2 1

Interior Holmes and Watson illustrations by Jeff Albrecht
Book design by Jason Zamajtuk and Scott Ciencin
Edited by Alice Alfonsi and Marc Cerasini

FOR MORE INFORMATION ABOUT
THE WATSON GUIDES™
Books, Learning Materials and Audios
(416) 483-3955
www.maddoxsmye.com

To our brothers, Dan Jr. and Marty.
Tops in their fields.
Tops with us.

—R&M

Table of Contents

Acknowledgments

What Michael Jordan Knows
(That Can Help You Sell More Cars)

You hold a book that will raise your income, increase your earnings potential—improve your life—if you learn and practice the secrets *we've* learned from the masters of selling cars. It can make you the Michael Jordan of car sales.

So ask yourself: Do you *want* to be the Michael Jordan of car sales?

You can do it. You just have to know what it takes.

And what is that, exactly? A good friend of ours—who also happens to be a twenty year car guy and a consistently top achieving salesperson—spelled out exactly what it takes to become the best in the world in any given field:

I went to see the Bulls play a few years ago with my son and two buddies. It was Michael Jordan's last week as an active player. We sat four rows behind the bench. It cost a grand apiece. $4,000 to see Michael Jordan play and it was worth it, because, after all, there's only one Michael Jordan.

The arena opened at 6:15 P.M. We got there at 6:20 P.M. There were only a 100 people in the stands because the game didn't start until 8:05 P.M.

We looked out and there on the court stood a six foot, six inch tall African-American guy wearing number 23. He was 13 feet from the basket and near him was a rack of 12 basketballs. One was missing: he was holding it. Then he was in action, taking turnaround jumpers.

He was Michael Jordan. It was unbelievable.

While every other member of the team was taping their ankles or drinking a soft drink or talking to his wife or looking at his contract, Michael Jordan was out there practicing, taking one turnaround jumper after another. We watched Michael Jordan take 40 minutes of turnaround jumpers before we even saw another guy with shorts and sneakers show up on the court. Michael Jordan practices 40 minutes of jumpers while everybody else is doing something different.

You tell me: If Michael Jordan thinks it's important enough to spend an extra 40 minutes practicing before the game, to strive to be better, then can any one of us tell ourselves that we don't need to work hard, we don't need to learn new skills, we don't need to look at any other market than the ones we know, and expect anyone to look at us as if we were the Michael Jordan of car sales?

You have to want it. You have to work at it. You have to keep practicing and learning. And you've got to have a plan.

So that's what we've created for you. This book is a blueprint for success using lessons from countless automotive industry top sellers to help *you* become the Michael Jordan of car salespeople!

Jump Start to Using This Book

The best thing about it is that while you *can* read it from cover-to-cover, you don't *have to*. This isn't a text book. Think of it instead as in interactive playbook. We've set this book up so that anyone can benefit from its strategies in minutes.

Take a look at the edge of the book. You'll see, when it's closed, that it looks something like a phone book. The gray boxes show you where each of the three parts start and stop.

PART ONE   PART TWO   PART THREE

Money   Mystery   Resources

The bookmark tabs on the top (see left) are for Editors' Notes, where you can get fast facts and instant, ready-to-use sales strategies.

On the page, Editors' Notes look like this (only bigger):

EDITORS' NOTES: WHAT WOMEN WANT
According to our studies, women are far more likely to respond positively to environments in which they are not treated exactly the same as men. The same amount of respect and consideration, yes, but in a selling or service environment, dealerships that take the particular needs and interests of women into consideration sell more cars to women and keep more women customers as return business. How can you tell what women want? Ask them. You won't regret it.   —R&M

The checkmark tabs on the top (see right) are for Chapter Checklists, where you can receive quick summaries of the key points made within each chapter.

A Chapter Checklist looks like this (only bigger):

Chapter Four Checklist

COMPETENCY EXPLORED IN THIS CHAPTER

Establish a Trusting Relationship.
Uncover Her Specific Needs and Wants.
Make A Professional Sales Presentation.
✓ **Complete A Pressure-less Closing.**
Build An Enhanced Relationship with Her and Hers.
Provide Efficient, Non-Intrusive Administration.

COMPETENCIES—*collections of observable behaviors in categories that, when demonstrated, indicate a level of successful performance.*

BEHAVIORS—*each competency is followed by a series of phrases that describe actions (or behaviors) characteristic of a person who performs with a high degree of ability in that area. The behaviors will be demonstrated, in varying degrees, by those with different abilities and positions.*

THINK

✓ Women sometimes need time to consider all the information they have been given. I should offer her a place where she can review the materials if necessary.

✓ She will give me all the information I need to close the deal *if I listen* to what she is saying and give her what she wants.

How to Get RICH Selling Cars to Women doesn't have to be read from start to finish, beginning on page one and moving one page to another. It's not a textbook. In the early stages of writing this book we asked accomplished salespersons to read the book and give us feedback. From their comments we learned different people respond very differently to the three parts of the book. Every salesperson had a "favorite" part, or way of learning the skills and behaviors.

Read just the mystery and pit your knowledge against the master detective Sherlock Holmes as he takes on the mystery of how to sell cars to women, or jump to the resource section and start practicing the competencies of the very best salesmen in the world. Or just flip through and read the editors' notes and the chapter summaries to get immediate tips and strategies. Approach this book in the way that's best for you.

As to the three parts, the break down is very simple: Part One: Don't Leave the Money on the Table, discusses where the automotive industry has been and where it is going, especially in regard to capturing the all-important women's market. You will gain valuable insight into why it is so important to sell to women and what kind of skills you will need to do so. Most importantly, it will fill you with a sense of pride about the role you play in the economy of our country.

Part Two: The Mystery, is very different. It is an actual story, one in which you put your existing knowledge and skills in the sales and service arena up against that of the legendary detective Sherlock Holmes and his biographer Dr. Watson. The mystery allows you to go along for the ride as you watch someone actually learn these skills and strategies and change the way they sell to women. And again, throughout this mystery, you will be rewarded with "Editors' Notes" that include tips, lessons, and statistics to help you master the art of selling cars to women-and getting rich in the process!

Part Three: Resources for Champion Salespeople gives you the inside track to three critical areas you will need to know to increase your sales to women: Why women want changes from car salespeople, the exact changes they want, and the method to making those lasting changes in your approach. In other words, "Why," "What," and "How."

Why: "The Voice of the Customer" section, taken from focus groups conducted by Sunny 95/WSNY 94.7FM (owned by Saga Communications, Inc.) the number-one rated women's radio station in Columbus, Ohio, will allow you to hear actual comments made by women customers about the car buying experience, their likes and dislikes, their wants and needs, and why they do or do not buy from you.

What: "The Six Competencies for Top Producers" section contains information for management as well as salespeople. The information in this section provides you with a blueprint of exactly what skills, behaviors, and attitudes you must master to become one of the best. This part will help you target what changes you and/or your team will need to make in order to improve your performance.

How: "Now That I Know What To Do...How Do I Do It?" gives you a guide for implementing the changes you want to make to become a top salesperson in the car business. This section is critically important, because we've all been to seminars where we've heard experts give what sounds like great advice at the time, *but*, when Monday morning rolls around, you're left wondering how to put all these new teachings into action. This chapter will assist you in understanding how we all makes changes in our life and the process that we all must work through in our quest to become the best of the best in our fields.

The vital information and all the lessons you will find within these pages, were compiled by Rebecca Maddox, the leading expert throughout the world in selling products and services to women, and Dr. Marti Smye, a world-renowned thought-leader in the field of change management. Millions of dollars and many years of painstaking effort have gone into gathering this information from the top salespeople in the automobile industry along with a variety of other related industries, so you can be assured that MaddoxSmye, LLC, are providing you with expert advice in how to reach this market.

Remember, what you learn in this book will benefit you professionally and personally. You will learn how to succeed financially by giving one of the most powerful markets exactly what they want!

Knowledge is power and you're about to become very powerful indeed.

PART ONE

DON'T LEAVE THE MONEY ON THE TABLE

Pride In The Industry

Pride.

A doctor saves a life in the emergency room. A lawyer argues a case masterfully and wins freedom for a wrongly accused man. A champion golfer plays the best game of his life and becomes a legend with his final stroke. When linked with accomplishments like this, a feeling of pride is not only acceptable, it's expected.

People working in the automotive industry also have good reason to take pride in what they do—and to take pride in the industry as a whole. The U.S. economy is driven by auto manufacturers, suppliers, and dealers. Consider these facts from the Alliance of Automobile Manufacturers:

✓ 6.6 million jobs stem directly from the auto industry.

✓ Seven "spin-off" jobs are created for every one worker directly employed by auto manufacturers.

✓ $243 billion is paid to auto employees each year.

✓ $74 billion enters the U.S. economy from automotive exports.

✓ Auto manufacturers throughout the U.S. are among the leading purchasers of aluminum, copper, iron, lead, plastics, rubber, textiles, vinyl, steel, and computer chips.

Picture what the world would be like if there were no auto industry, if the greatest single industry linked to manufacturing and the biggest generator of retail business and employment worldwide suddenly closed up shop. The impact on the global economy would be catastrophic.

What does it all come down to? What is the fuel that keeps this incredible world-spanning income-generating machine operating? Simple. It's the dedicated and hard-working individuals who are out there every day selling and servicing cars at dealerships across the U.S.

It's you.

Every time you meet and greet a customer, every time you make a sale or score a high mark on a customer satisfaction index, you help cement another brick in the wall that is our nation's economy, the wall that keeps us free and strong in today's global marketplace.

According to NADA statistics, 17.2 million vehicles were sold in 2001. That's over $500 billion in new car sales in the U.S. alone!

NADA further informs us that you are one of 228,900 car salespeople in the United States.

Many dealers expect a performance level—on average—of 10 cars per month. Let's say that's how many cars *you* are already selling monthly. Imagine the impact on your personal pay if you sold even one more car a month from reading this book and learning these skills. And consider what 12 more car sales per year would do for your annual income. It all boils down to a performance and pay increase of 10% annually. Not a bad raise these days.

Now...imagine what would happen across the country if every car salesperson, all 228,900 strong, experienced a similar 10% increase in performance and sales. That would result in 2,746,800 more cars being sold each year.

Your job is vitally important. You and the automotive industry make an enormous difference in the world economy and the lives of individuals and all our communities on the home front each and every day.

The additional sales we're discussing would mean hundreds, if not thousands of people employed across the U.S. and around the globe manufacturing those cars as well as processing the materials needed to make those cars (like aluminum, copper, iron, lead, plastics, rubber, textiles, vinyl, steel and computer chips). This doesn't even include the people employed making spare parts for those new cars or the people who service and repair those cars (don't forget about the service people who number 325,800 in the U.S. and generated revenues of $80 billion in 2001).

We've shown you, beyond any shadow of a doubt, that you and the auto industry make an enormous difference in our economy every day. And if you knew there was a way to feel even more empowered, to strengthen this industry, and to bolster your own bottom line—if someone showed you a new field to conquer, a new source of revenue right in front of you, would you listen—or turn away?

The fact is 80% of all automotive purchases are directly made or influenced by women, yet so many people believe that selling to women (and service is sales, never forget that) is some unbelievably difficult mystery, no one could possibly crack. Not true.

The women's market is the key to that 10% increase, and that increase is only the beginning.

Increasing your performance and sales will have a positive "domino effect" on your local economy and ultimately on the world. You *should* take pride in that. And taking pride in what you do, and in this industry, translates to confidence. Your confidence, your attitude, your pride is what you reflect to the rest of the world and your customers.

Pride is key to your ability to succeed everyday. You have to go to work believing in what you do, believing you are honorable and that the higher your personal income grows, the more good you are doing for the economy. With pride, you know that your potential, the joint potential of all 228,000 salespeople in the auto industry and the industry itself, is unlimited. Your pride, and the confidence it will help you project, will have an incalculable impact on your ability to sell more.

Pride is about always doing your best...just like Michael Jordan. He took pride in the sport of basketball and in the team he was playing for.

If you have both, you will be unbeatable.

You are a professional. Your actions impact on the world. Take *pride*...and use it to get rich selling cars to women!

Shouldn't We Just Treat Her Like A Man?

There are people alive today who lived through a time when women did not have the right to vote, when women did not receive equal pay for equal work, when women's job opportunities were few and far-between, or outright demeaning. Times have changed. Attitudes have changed.

In today's PC age, equality is the buzzword. Ask most people in sales or service if they treat women the same as men and they will proudly answer, "Absolutely!"

Yet therein lies the problem. Of course women want and deserve the same rights and opportunities as men. But to ignore the obvious distinctions in the way men and women are socialized, the very separate and distinct needs, wants, and mind sets that make women different from men is, in essence, to ignore an incredible financial opportunity.

The women's market is like a tidal wave perched over a city, a powerful and unrelenting force that must be met head on, and those with the courage to do so will find themselves awash with riches. The key to selling any product to women is understanding and celebrating their differences from men. Your sales pitch and follow-through service must display the special knowledge and skills women customers value.

You might be shaking your head right now and thinking: This doesn't apply to me. This isn't even true. I've *asked* women if they want to be treated differently and they themselves have answered, "Oh, no. Absolutely not."

If that's happened to you, there's a reason. Women today are actively discouraged from speaking out on this topic. They are told "different" means "less than equal" or "looking for special treatment." And oftentimes, women perceive the question of, "Well, *don't* you want to be treated the same as a man?" as a leading one (in other words, one in which the desired answer is implied in the question itself—a further discouragement to speaking their minds, and the *truth*.)

Here's a study in contrasts for you: A couple we know is getting married. The groom-to-be went to the first "Tux-R-Us" outlet he could find He could have cared less how brusque or distracted the *salesperson* who waited on him was. He "got the whole thing over with" as quickly as possible so he could get home in time for a football game he was going to watch with his buddies.

But his bride-to-be had a different story to tell. When she went shopping for her wedding dress, she drove from store-to-store and found several outlets in which the salespeople treated her well, but the dresses she tried on simply didn't do the trick. Finally, at her last stop, she found the wedding dress of her dreams. Unfortunately, the salesperson was condescending and rude to her.

Unfortunate for the salesperson, that is.

Our friend took down all the information on the dress, walked out the door, and returned to one of the stores she had previously visited. She handed all the particulars to one of the salespeople who had treated her with respect and had listened to her wants and needs. The salesperson special ordered the dress—and got the sale.

The moral of the story is simple: If a woman doesn't like the way she's being treated, she probably won't take a salesperson on the side and complain. But she WILL walk.

So, to answer the question from the beginning of this section: Shouldn't we just treat her like a man? The answer is: *absolutely not.* Remember, when a woman customer comes into your store, she's not just shopping for a particular product, she's also looking to form a long-term buying relationship. She may have already been to some of your competitors and she may have an opinion of their product and the quality of their sales and service. But even if she thinks highly of another salesperson or dealership, she's come to you because she's hoping you will outshine anyone and anything she's seen before. And even if all goes well, she may leave, look elsewhere, *and come back to you.* Why? It's simple: Women have the phrase "it pays to shop around" drilled into them from an early age.

If you treat her with respect and give your all during the sales process, she will not only choose to give you her business time and time again, but she will also recommend you to all her friends.

Just in Case You Didn't Know...

Women Represent 51% of U.S. Population

Women 108,133,727
Men   100,004,367

(Over 18 Years of Age)

Source: U.S. Census Bureau, Census 2000

Why ignore over half the population?

Women Marital Statistics

The majority of adult women—5.3 out of every 10—are married. Which means, conversely, that almost *half* are single.

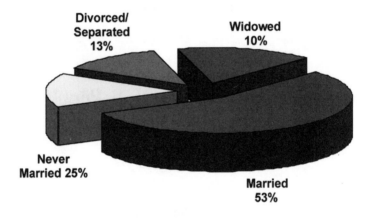

Source: Census Bureau's Marital Status and Living Arrangements: 2000

Don't assume every woman lives in a "traditional" family.

Women-Owned Single Family Homes

More than 57% of single women are now homeowners.

2000	**2005***
16.4 million	**17.2 million**

*Projection

Single women make major purchases.

Women's Personal Earnings

64 million women work outside the home for pay
(58 million in 1996).

13.5 (10) million earn > $30,000/year.
6.5 (2.4) million earn > $50,000/year.

99% of all women will work for pay at some time in
their life.

Women can afford to buy your cars.

Women-Owned Businesses

Women own 38% of the businesses in the United states resulting in over 9 million women-owned businesses that employ 27.5 million people and have $3.6 trillion in revenue.

Women employ more people than the Fortune 500.

Today, Women Own or Control Real Wealth

Women represent 47% of all investors

Women own over 53% of all stocks

43% of all individuals with assets of $500,000 or more are women.

Over next 20 years $20 trillion dollars will be inherited by baby boomers.

Women live 5.4 years longer than men.

Women have their own money and selling to women can make you rich.

Hours Women Spend on the Job

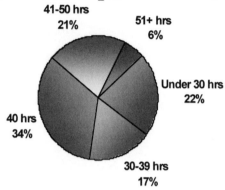

Weekly Hours Spent at Work by Employed Women

Women are out of time.

Internet Usage

1996
Internet Users:

MEN	WOMEN
82%	18%

2000
Internet Users:

MEN	WOMEN
50%	50%

Women use the Internet as much as men.

Men & Women Use The Internet Differently

MEN

Check sports, news, stocks
Build web pages
Download software or music
Play games

WOMEN

Email friends
Research
Shop
Conduct transactions

Women do the research, so assume they know the product and what they want.

Major Areas of Gender Differences

1. Communications
     How we talk to each other.

2. Connections
     How we develop trust and relationships.

3. Decisions
     How we decide what we are going to do.

4. Listening
     How and what we hear.

To sum it all up...

You can't treat her the same as a man.

PART TWO

THE MYSTERY

The Business Consultants Meet The Consulting Detectives

Everyday wisdom and common sense solutions can come from the strangest places. We've given countless talks throughout the world on the important skills needed to sell to the women's market. Wherever we've gone, people have asked us to put what we know into a book. As it turns out, a certain well known physician beat us to the punch!

This manuscript was sent to us by a client whose hobby is collecting old and rare books. Experts have evaluated the weathered pages mailed to us and opinions vary. We believe it truly came from the talented hand of the brilliant surgeon who chronicled (and participated in) the adventures of the world's greatest detective.

One thing's undeniable—the author knows his stuff. Women make up the *majority* of car buyers today. Yet the mystery remains of how to reach them, how to make that sale every time, and how to keep them as life-long customers.

It's time for that mystery to be solved. The ageless truths and wisdom contained in these pages will elevate you from the ranks of the everyday sales or serviceperson, transforming you into a master detective of the automotive world. Enjoy, as we did, this little book with its mammoth rewards, and gain the competitive edge you need to make a killing each month—by selling cars to women!

Rebecca Maddox & Marti Smye

Chapter One
An Unsolvable Riddle?

From the journal of
Dr. John H. Watson

"Automobiles!" Holmes exclaimed, hurling the latest edition of *The Strand* to the floor. "Is there no getting away from them?"

Frowning, I picked up the magazine, glancing at the advertisement that had angered Holmes. It was for a car I didn't recognize, though I was now seeing so many on the streets that I was certain I would soon be able to identify this particular make and model at a glance.

A car horn honked in the distance, beyond our comfortable sitting room at 221B Baker Street. Holmes frowned as if he truly believed the sound had set out to mock him.

"Cars *are* the future," I said softly.

"First electric lights, now this," Holmes muttered, dropping heavily into his chair. "Who do they think will buy these horrible contraptions?"

"Ah, well...*men*, of course," I said, gesturing at the advertisement. "It's clear that's who they're trying to reach."

Holmes settled back, a wry, triumphant smile creasing his hawklike face. "Then *that* will be their undoing."

I sighed and went to the window. Our world was changing rapidly, there could be no doubt of that. And Holmes was no longer the young man he had been when we first met. The dawn of the twentieth century and the arrival of the Industrial Age had brought change to a time he'd spent a lifetime studying. Rather than seeing an opportunity to explore a bold *new world*, he met every technological advancement as if it were an annoyance. I worried for him. "Why do you say that selling strictly to men will be this emerging industry's undoing?" I asked.

"Their *ultimate* undoing," Holmes said.

"*Who* would you propose they sell to? Children? Like our Baker Street Irregulars?"

Holmes sighed and waved his hand magnanimously. "Watson, again you miss the obvious. You know my methods. Apply them."

I already had a good idea of exactly where he was going with this. I often did, but to tell him so would have defeated the purpose of the exercise.

"*Women*, Watson. Women are the key..."

Now it was my turn to sigh, though I did so inwardly. Women? What did Sherlock Holmes know of women? Their role in our society and the power they wielded had changed radically in recent years, but my friend's view of them was the same as ever. He was unaware of their achievements, oblivious to their potential. The days of the weeping governess or the indecisive flirt were long gone. Dealing with women in this day and age required a set of tools—and a far greater range of perception—than I feared my dear friend capable of ever attaining.

"Very well, Holmes," I said, nodding, looking right at him, and leaning forward as if I were hanging on his every word. It was a trick I had learned early on to induce him to part with information. A trick, or I should say a *technique*, that also came in handy in my dealings as a married man.

Another, I will freely admit, I learned from Holmes himself: Maintain eye contact at all times. The benefits of this lesson have always been substantial, and I've found it amusing that Holmes learned the trick from speaking with actors!

EDITORS' NOTES: EYE ON THE PRIZE
When talking with a customer face-to-face, do you find it difficult to maintain eye contact for long periods of time? *Suggestion*: **don't look in both of the customer's eyes, choose just one eye and keep your gaze locked on it. This way you will be able to maintain eye contact for long periods without your own eyes getting tired and darting around (which makes you appear shifty.)**   **—R&M**

"Tell me, Holmes," I said, "how would you go about selling cars to women—and why do you feel it is so important?"

Holmes leaned back, his brow furrowed, his eyes attaining a faraway look. "As to the latter, that should be self-evident," he began. "Most men who have fallen under the beguiling spell of the opposite sex base practically all their actions on making themselves seem more appealing to their prospective conquests. A flashy new *expensive* toy such as an automobile can show how well off these men are—how easily they can provide riches. Hence, by piquing the interest of women in these contraptions, men can easily meet their goal of impressing their intended conquests.

"In the case of a married or otherwise entangled male, such a hapless creature will do everything in his power to maintain the interest of his partner, thus keeping her from straying. Hence, once again, a purchase aimed at arresting the attention of the fair sex must first be coveted by women."

I could not prevent a low growl of disapproval from escaping my lips. Holmes' theory was ridiculous! It gave women no credit and painted them as empty-headed vessels in need of shiny bright baubles to keep them happy.

Holmes went on, oblivious to my displeasure.

"As to selling to them—" he continued, but I quickly cut him off.

"You're not talking about selling to *women* at all," I exclaimed. "You're saying that by appealing strictly to a man's vanity, or to his sense of competitiveness with his male peers, by not taking into account his dealings with his *sweetheart*, the automobile industry will fail in the long run."

"Yes," Holmes said, closing his eyes as if imagining something highly pleasurable. "And I will have quiet on my streets once more."

This was too much. "Holmes, you act as if a woman wouldn't—or couldn't—make such a purchase on her own, for reasons of her own."

My friend smiled sadly. "Naturally, there will be exceptions, if only to prove the rule. But I think these would be few and far between."

"Face it, Holmes, you haven't the first clue as to how to solve this mystery."

He opened his eyes, appearing most unhappy at having his daydream disrupted. "You would actually have me waste my talents and energies designing a sales campaign targeting women? They're clearly nothing more than a minuscule, middling *niche* market!"

I stood up, preparing to take my leave. There was only so much of this balderdash I could take. "Holmes, were you to take the time to investigate, you would learn that women influence or exert outright control over eighty percent of all purchases made today."

"If that is true, and I would love to see upon what data you base such a statement, then I am fortunate to be a detective, and *not* a salesman."

"It *is* true," I said, "and it accounts for why you have not had a case in three months." I pointed at the door. "No woman wishes to cross that threshold and be treated by you as if she were living in another age!"

EDITORS' NOTES: FACTS AND FIGURES

Was Watson right about his facts and figures? According to 2000 census data, women make up 50.9% of the U.S. population. Why would anyone selling anything willingly ignore over half of the population? As to Holmes' earlier statement about women not being able to make purchases on their own, that's certainly not the case today.

Many women, married or not, earn their own money. In fact, 64 million women work outside the home, with 13.5 million earning over $30,000 a year, and 6.5 million earning over $50,000 a year. Most importantly, women now buy 52% of new cars ($81 billion worth), and, as Watson said, women influence over 80% of all vehicle purchases.

Holmes should listen up, because the good doctor knows his stuff, and he's the guy _we're_ listening to!   —R&M

Just then a knock came at the door, and Mrs. Hudson appeared. "Mr. Holmes, you have a caller waiting downstairs."

Holmes arched an eyebrow. "A client?"

"I would say so, judging from the frantic way I was spoken to."

"Frantic," Holmes repeated happily. "You see? To whom else would that word be applied? It is a woman in need of my services!"

Mrs. Hudson narrowed her gaze. "I didn't say—"

"No need to belabor the point, dear Mrs. Hudson," Holmes said, his eyes alight with excitement at the prospect of having what he considered a proper mystery in which to delve. He didn't notice the way Mrs. Hudson flinched at his dismissive tone, or how her shoulders tightened at the use of the word "dear."

"If you would let me finish," Mrs. Hudson said.

"You are too kind, but there is no need, *sweet woman*," Holmes went on, digging himself in deeper with each word. I half-expected Mrs. Hudson to take the old-fashioned silver receiving tray, upon which our caller's card had been placed, and hit him upside the head with it!

"Holmes, you might take a moment and listen, rather than interrupt," I said. "You do realize that you aren't listening at all. You are simply ignoring what's being said while you wait to speak."

My friend looked my way, unperturbed. "My apologies, Watson, did you say something?"

Mrs. Hudson heatedly dropped the tray on a table by the door, and spun in her tracks—then jumped back

Illustration Number One: Ignoring
Poor Sherlock. He thinks he knows how to treat women.
*Mrs. Hudson clearly doesn't agree. Holmes is in the **ignoring** stage of change. He does not recognize that there is a problem. But he will soon!*

as a thin mustached man in a wrinkled suit burst into the room. He clumsily brushed past Mrs. Hudson, who shook her head in displeasure as she stormed out of the room.

"Mr. Holmes? Mr. Sherlock Holmes?" the man said, his eyes wide, his tone ringing with desperation. "My name is Herbert George Wells—and I need your help!"

Holmes appeared vexed. "Not a woman at all," he murmured. "Though he seems as emotional as one…"

Now it was my turn to restrain myself from applying the nearest weighty object to the back of the detective's skull. He had much to learn about women, and for some reason, I had a sense that our approaching adventure would present him with the opportunity to do just that.

What Holmes would do with such an opportunity, however, I had no idea.

"Tell me," Holmes said, studying the man, "this wouldn't have anything to do with those beastly contraptions known as automobiles, would it? And women?"

Wells practically leaped back in surprise. "How could you possibly know that?"

"Come," Holmes said, gesturing at a waiting chair. "Tell us everything."

Chapter One Checklist

COMPETENCY EXPLORED IN THIS CHAPTER

✓ **Establish a Trusting Relationship.**
Uncover Her Specific Needs and Wants.
Make A Professional Sales Presentation.
Complete a Pressure-less Closing.
Build an Enhanced Relationship with Her and Hers.
Provide Efficient, Non-Intrusive Administration.

COMPETENCIES—*collections of observable behaviors in categories that, when demonstrated, indicate a level of successful performance.*

BEHAVIORS—*each competency is followed by a series of phrases that describe actions (or behaviors) characteristic of a person who performs with a high degree of ability in that area. The behaviors will be demonstrated, in varying degrees, by those with different abilities and positions.*

KEEP IN MIND

✓ Women make up more than half the U.S. population.

✓ More women buy cars then men. In fact, 52% of all vehicles are purchased by women.

✓ Women are responsible for buying and/or influencing the purchase of 8 out of 10 cars sold.

THINK

✓ The woman considers me untrustworthy. I have to prove that I *am* trustworthy. Trust is not given easily or automatically. It must be earned.

SAY

✓ How can I be most helpful to you today?

✓ What's your name? How would you like to be addressed?

✓ Would you like to walk around by yourself, look at what we have to offer, and contact me when you have a question? I could check back with you in 5-10 minutes to see if you need anything. Or would you like me to accompany you around the showroom?

✓ Would you tell me about your past car-buying experiences? What was good or bad about those prior experiences?

DO

When approaching a woman customer:

✓ Walk tall and confidently.

✓ Reach out to shake the woman's hand when you first meet her.

✓ *Smile.* Be positive when introducing yourself to the customer. For example, "Good morning! My name's John Smith. How can I be most helpful to you today?"

During the sales encounter:

✓ **If she only wants information, give her what she asks for;** then offer your card and ask her to contact you when she is ready to make her car purchase.

✓ **Be succinct when responding to questions.**

✓ **Be respectful of her time.**

✓ *Listen well to her concerns.* Clarify any misunderstandings. Find ways to improve this buying experience for her in every way possible.

✓ **Lean forward, into the conversation, to show** you're listening and to demonstrate your interest in what the customer has to say.

✓ *Send the right non-verbal cues.* When meeting a customer for the first time, make sure your body language says you are open and glad to see them. Keep your arms at your sides, not crossed in front of your chest or hidden behind your back.

✓ *Maintain Eye Contact.* The secret to maintaining eye contact for long stretches of time is to choose only one of the customer's eyes and stare into it. Otherwise, your flickering gaze may make you appear impatient or untrustworthy to the customer.

DON'T

✓ Use a dismissive tone.

✓ Act superior.

✓ Cut women off in mid-sentence.

✓ Call the woman "sweetie," "honey," and so on.

✓ Assume she is not the decision-maker.

✓ Equate her knowledge about cars with intelligence and ability.

✓ Ask about her spouse or significant other unless she brings up the topic.

Chapter Two

A Profitable Encounter

In all the years I had known Sherlock Holmes, one thing had become abundantly clear to me. All that truly mattered to him was the pursuit of excellence in his chosen field and the precise and firm application of justice in an all-too unjust world.

I also knew H.G. Wells. Or, I should say, I knew *of* him. Wells was a noted futurist and commentator on society, producing more than the fanciful tales for which he had gained a good deal of popularity. For my taste, "The History of Mr. Polly" was vastly preferable to *The War of the Worlds*.

"How can we help you?" I asked.

Wells held out his hand. "My name is Herbert George—"

"We know who you are," Holmes said, ignoring the hand Wells offered. I moved to shake the man's hand, but was too late.

Wells withdrew his handkerchief and wiped his face. He was sweaty from exertion, and it was clear he had run at least part of the way to get here. But there were clearly other factors contributing to Wells' agitated state than mere physical strain.

I sighed. A friendly greeting, a simple handshake, might have gone a long way in relieving his mental state.

EDITORS' NOTES: MEET, GREET AND IMPRESS

We teach salespeople how to shake hands and greet customers properly, but we don't share these valuable lessons with our service personnel. Why not? It occurred to us that the last time we were at the service desk of a car dealership, the service personnel didn't shake hands or greet us very well. Their stance was more, "Okay, what's your problem?" (But in a nice way.) Remember—service *is* sales, no ifs, ands, or buts about it!

> *Suggestion*: Every service person should attend and master a sales training course. These classes include great "how to" information about greeting customers properly when they come in, and thanking them for their patronage when they leave.   —R&M

I repeated my question: "How can we help you, Mr. Wells?"

Before Wells could answer, Holmes gestured theatrically and said, "Watson, that should be obvious. We should call Mrs. Hudson and get the man a pitcher of ice water to *soak* his *head*. If we don't, he may keel over on the spot, and the world will be deprived of more of his 'literary' ranting."

"Holmes, really!" I cried.

Wells' gaze grew hard. "I suppose I should apply your vaunted method of observation and deduce that my presence here is unwelcome *despite* my circumstances."

"Not at all," Holmes said dryly, "it is indeed a pleasure to entertain the author of such *fair* and *unbiased* treatises on the Victorian social order as 'The New Utopia.' Personally, I found the old one pleasant enough."

Now, I understood the reason for Holmes' enmity. Wells was of the future, Holmes a part of the past. Everything Holmes loathed in our modern world was enthusiastically embraced by Wells, and the system that had supported Holmes was one Wells found abhorrent.

Wells scowled. "We may have our differences in opinion, Mr. Holmes, but I was told—"

"Holmes, a word if I may," I said, quickly drawing my friend away from the flushed and furious Wells. "Your first client in three months and you're going to drive him out that door."

"And where would he go? Some *other* detective agency? Hah!"

I waited for Holmes to read the lack of amusement in my visage.

The fire went out of him. "Yes, in this day and age, I suppose he might do just that."

EDITORS' NOTES: CAR PURCHASE

A car is a commodity purchase, albeit a big one. If women don't like the way they are being treated by you, they will walk. Unlike the way it used to be, women have more choices regarding who to buy a car from. They buy from salespeople they like, salespeople who exhibits certain desired behaviors. **—R&M**

"You must try to be pleasant, Holmes. This is a professional encounter. So *be professional.*"

"To a man whose views I abhor, a man with whom I have absolutely nothing in common?"

"If you want his business, then yes."

"Are you suggesting that I must *sell* myself and my services?" He gestured at the advertisement for cars in *The Strand* magazine lying on the floor. "That I should perform as if I were attempting to sell him one of those devilish devices?"

"Exactly so," I said firmly. "And more importantly, try to put yourself in his shoes. He *had* to know a meeting with someone opposed to everything he believes in might go badly, and yet Wells came anyway. What does that say to you about the man and the dire nature of his situation?"

"Of course," Holmes said at last. "When attempting to ferret out the motivation of a villain, I've tried to see the world as a criminal might. It hadn't occurred to me to do so with someone like Wells."

"It is something to be done for everyone who walks in our door. I learned that not only in my training and experience as a healer, but also by watching you."

"Emotion is not our guide," stated Holmes. "We must proceed under the cool light of reason."

"Reason and *empathy*, Holmes," I said. "Especially empathy."

EDITORS' NOTES: TOP PRIORITY

We simply can't resist commending Watson on his insights and technique. He understands that in *any* first encounter we want to count as profitable, a great amount of care must be taken to make the person we're meeting feel comfortable and confident that they've made the right choice by coming to us.

Be in the moment, focused firmly on the here and now, ask open-ended questions gather knowledge whenever possible. Consider this checklist of precision listening techniques:

✓ Listen fully without interrupting.

✓ Give feedback to the speaker on what was *said*, not on what you *think* the speak er might have *meant*.

✓ Obtain relevant details by asking open-ended questions (no question that can be answered through a simple yes/no) and listen with the intent of using the information.

✓ If you are unclear on what the speaker meant, clarify by reflecting the speaker's statement. "I want to make sure I understand. What you want is…"

✓Always reach agreement on the next step to take.

✓ Demonstrate listening by taking notes.

Lead on, Watson!   **—R&M**

We went back to Wells, who had become temporarily distracted by Holmes' vast collection of reference books.. Wells cited a particular volume he had read about but had never before laid eyes on, and Holmes graciously offered to loan it to the fellow. It was as close to an apology as Holmes could get, and I was grateful to see the two men put aside their differences and get on with business.

Wells quickly explained that he had been robbed, or so he had deduced. The only copy of a highly valued manuscript that Wells had spent months preparing was missing—and so was his assistant. The coincidence was too great to be ignored.

"So you believe he may try to sell this manuscript?" I ventured.

"He may try to pass it off as his own work," Wells said worriedly. "All the notes for the book are in his handwriting because I spoke them aloud and he wrote them down for me. And the concepts involved were discussed with no one else, not even my publisher."

"Earlier you said this matter had something to do with the automobile business," I said.

"Yes." He suddenly appeared quite stricken.

"Actually, Watson," Holmes interrupted. "I was the one who made that observation. I noted motor oil beneath his fingertips, stains of paint commonly used on such contraptions speckled upon his trousers, and a scuffing to his shoes involving patterns particular to motorcar manufacturing plants."

"It seems you have me at that," Wells said.

"Perhaps Mr. Wells is reluctant to discuss the content of the manuscript for fear of having his ideas further pirated," Holmes said. "You are, after all, a well-known author in your own right, Watson."

I looked to Wells. "You may rely on my discretion. No mention of this case will be made in print during either of our lifetimes, unless you so will it."

Wells nodded. "My reticence was foolish. How can you find a manuscript when you don't even know what it concerns? Automobiles, yes. They are, you see, the *future*. And that's what my manuscript is about. Automobiles and their chief buyers—*women*. It is my definitive vision of the future, and the roles both will play in it. So, you see, there are markets aplenty for the knowledge in this book. Stock market speculators first and foremost. "

Holmes stood up. "I'm in agreement with you, Wells. If you have turned your quarters upside down already—"

"I have," Wells interjected. "The book is nowhere to be found."

"Then your assistant is the likely culprit," Holmes said. "Tell us all you can about him."

Sheepishly, Wells removed a folded sheet of paper from his jacket pocket and handed it to Holmes. "This address—it's all I know of him. He rooms here, or so he said. I've never had occasion to spend time with him outside of work."

"I quite understand," Holmes said, ushering the worried writer to the door.

"As to your fee—"

"We'll work out mutually agreeable terms after this mystery is solved. We have your card and will be in touch as soon as we have news."

Wells nodded and quietly departed.

After the echo of his footfalls faded down the stairs, Holmes looked at me.

"So, Watson. How would you evaluate my performance?"

"I would say you're learning already, Holmes. And gaining knowledge is *always* a profitable enterprise."

We left for the address Wells had given us, unaware that we were about to encounter a far greater challenge than the one we had just faced: The locked room, and within it, our first clues to the role *the woman* would play in this adventure.

Chapter Two Checklist

COMPETENCY EXPLORED IN THIS CHAPTER

Establish a Trusting Relationship.
✓ Uncover Her Specific Needs and Wants.
Make A Professional Sales Presentation.
Complete a Pressure-less Closing.
Build an Enhanced Relationship with Her and Hers.
Provide Efficient, Non-Intrusive Administration.

COMPETENCIES—*collections of observable behaviors in categories that, when demonstrated, indicate a level of successful performance.*

BEHAVIORS—*each competency is followed by a series of phrases that describe actions (or behaviors) characteristic of a person who performs with a high degree of ability in that area. The behaviors will be demonstrated, in varying degrees, by those with different abilities and positions.*

THINK

✓ Did I show her that I will treat her better than other car salespeople have treated her in the past? I consider it a challenge to get on her good side.

✓ How can I get to know the customer and her needs so I can better serve her? I should slow down the process and take a little more time now to get information so I can save both of us a lot of time later.

✓ Did I actively listen to the customer as if she were a generous heiress deciding if I was worthy of a major monetary bequest?

✓ *Men and Women are different.* Did I understand the gender differences and how a woman's individual buying processes may be different from mine?

✓ *Did I respect her efforts?* What can I do to demonstrate that respect? Women do a great deal of research before buying a car. I should conduct myself like a trusted advisor through the sales process, adding information when requested and when necessary.

SAY

✓ What research have you done on cars? Do you have any questions?

✓ What will the car be used for?

✓ What is important to you in a car? Safety? Reliability? Gas Mileage? Warrantee? Let me know so I can guide you toward one that will best fit your needs.

DO

✓ **Ask** her open-ended questions (who, what, where, when, why) to find out what she wants.

✓ **Perform** a needs appraisal to identify what car is best for her requirements.

✓ *Keep a firm grip on things.* Consider attending classes that teach you the proper way to greet a customer, with special attention to a firm handshake.

✓ **Recommend**, but do not insist on a test drive. For example, "If you have time today, would you like to take a test drive?"

✓ **Put** the control for talking about money squarely with her. For example, "Do you have a monthly target amount? Or do you want to talk about that after further investigating your options?"

DON'T

✓ *Assume anything.* A woman on her own is very likely to have sole buying power, and a woman who enters the dealership with a man may just be bringing a male friend for moral support.

✓ **Slouch** when approaching a woman customer: it can make you look shifty or defeated, like you've given up before you've even gotten started.

✓ *Put your hands where they don't belong.* Avoid distracting gestures and touching the customer.

Chapter Three

The Locked Room

If you have read my previous account, "The Scandal in Bohemia," you are well aware that Holmes gave the moniker "the woman" to only one female, the former opera singer and adventurer Irene Adler. That, of course, was Holmes' choice. For my purposes, there is another woman who earned that title—Lysette Price.

We would not meet Miss Price until passing several more trials, but it was at the boarding house where Jonathan Dooley, Wells' missing assistant, had been staying that we first discovered Miss Price's connection to the case.

We wished to reach the boarding house as quickly as possible, but Holmes firmly resisted the opportunity to travel by automobile. There were still a few horse-drawn Hansom cabs in London, though their numbers were diminishing. We caught one and were soon bouncing about on its hard wooden seats.

Holmes was uncomplaining as the carriage clattered down the cobblestone street. In fact, the particular rhythms of this ride were like those of history to him—familiar, safe, and comforting. I, on the other hand, had ridden in enough cars to vastly prefer the smoother ride that automobiles provided. Holmes disagreed, of course. Upon seeing a driver awkwardly jerking his car into traffic, Holmes smiled with wicked delight as a man on the street hollered, "Get a horse!"

The boarding house was unremarkable—a two-story building with shuttered windows and a walk-up leading to the front door. We had visited such edifices countless times, yet Holmes stood staring for long moments. Yet there was something different about Holmes on this occasion. He glanced at the street once the Hansom had departed, his expression revealing something unfamiliar, the look of a sleepwalker who was only now awakening, becoming aware in altogether alien circumstances.

The world was changing and I believed he sensed then and there that he must change with it, too, or risk being left behind. Was he up for the task? I knew that he was more than capable, but there was a difference between being able to do a thing, and *willing* to do a thing. I believe by now he grasped the importance of making the effort, but his old beliefs were difficult to overcome.

"This way, Holmes," I said gently, nudging his arm, guiding him in the direction of the boarding house.

He laughed, shrugging off my hand. "Do not mistake my engaging in my craft for anything else. I was taking in our surroundings, Watson, immersing myself in the world that our young Mr. Dooley visited each night when he returned from his gainful employment."

"Of course," I said, stepping aside as Holmes strode confidently toward the boarding house.

A young man with red hair and freckles answered the front door on the third knock. He might have been fourteen, no older. Holmes straightened up immediately, his chin rising, his eyes crackling with fire. "Please tell Mr. Dooley that two old acquaintances are here to see him."

"Dooley?" the young man asked. "He's not here."

"Then show us to his room, and we shall wait for him."

Holmes' voice was so commanding that the red-haired lad frowned unhappily but showed us in anyway, leading us up the stairs to the second floor landing, then taking us to the locked door of Dooley's room.

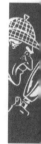

The lad was fishing in his pockets for the proper key, when a woman's voice rang out.

"Ronald? What mischief are you up to?"

The lad started as a dark-haired woman in her forties emerged from the room next door and immediately fixed him with a look of displeasure.

Her face was kind, her features pleasing. I sensed her strong will and independent spirit, along with an openness and intelligence that did not surprise me in the least. This encounter, I was certain, would be a beneficial one—provided the woman was *treated* with respect.

"Dear lady," Holmes said with a 'reassuring' tone one might use only when addressing a frightened and helpless child, "do you not have other duties to which you might attend? This fine lad has matters firmly in hand, I assure you. Do let us get on with it."

The woman's nostrils flared and her eyes widened as her ire became apparent. I sensed at once that Holmes' air of superiority was likely to crush any chance we may have had in gaining entrance to the locked room.

"I am Emily Bradley, and this is my house," she said firmly. "That boy works for me, and I don't know either of you. Explain yourselves, or be prepared to be forcibly ejected from these premises."

"You are the lady of the house," Holmes said wearily. "Is the *man* not available?"

The red-haired lad made a dash for it, citing his many chores to excuse his hasty departure.

"So you want the *man* of the house," Emily stated, her arms behind her, wrists clasped as she swept our way. "There *are* men here. Shall I introduce you?"

"Such would be my preference," Holmes said.

"Very well."

She led us to the end of the corridor, where she knocked on another door. In moments, an old man in a safari outfit answered, a blunderbuss in his wrinkled hands, a look of alarm in his crinkled visage. The handful of white hairs that clung determinedly to his shiny pate stood straight up, and his eyes were wild.

"Is it pheasant season already?" he asked, his voice breaking with hope. He held up the blunderbuss. "I have old Bessy here loaded for bear. Or mongoose. Or ostrich. Whatever is in season!"

Holmes grimaced, easing the door closed, the old man sounding off in displeasure as he disappeared within. Holmes looked the woman straight in the eye. "Madame, I assure you, we are here on a matter of the utmost urgency and importance."

"For *you*, perhaps," she replied. "It seems to me, however, that you have need of something only *I* can give you, yet you seem unwilling to pay me even the most common of courtesies."

Holmes became flustered. "Good woman, may I appeal to your inherently forgiving nature and ask you to grant us access to the room of master Dooley, as we—"

"Inherently *what* nature?" she asked, barely restraining a laugh. "You know *nothing* of me. How in blazes would you have the first inkling as to what is or is not inherent in my nature?"

Holmes chuckled. "You are a woman, after all, and there are certain constants in this universe. The earth spirals around the sun, seasons change as they must, and women—"

I could take no more. "My name is doctor John H. Watson, and my companion is Mr. Sherlock Holmes, consulting detective."

"For a detective, he should bloody well get a clue!" Emily roared.

"That is precisely what we are *here* to *do*," Holmes entreated.

I stepped forward. "Emily—may I call you Emily?"

"As I observe a wedding band upon your finger and I can plainly see that your lack of patience with your companion rivals my own, I will allow it, yes," Emily replied.

I had noticed the wedding band upon her finger the moment she had entered the hall, as I'm sure, did Holmes. But I refused to gravitate toward any definitive conclusions regarding her current marital status or her

Illustration Number Two: Attending
*Hmmm...Is it possible that Holmes really does have a lot to learn about how women want to be treated? You bet! But Sherlock is only in the **attending** stage of change. He sees the need for change, but continues with his current behaviors.*

ability—or inability—to help us based on that single bit of evidence. She could be a widow for all I knew, or perhaps she wore the ring to fend off unwanted advances. I have known men who have done the same. One thing was clear to me—take nothing for granted. I could assume only that care must be taken at every turn when dealing with this woman whose patience had already been tried by the insistent demands and lofty attitude my friend had exhibited.

"If I may make some observations of my own," Holmes said, barreling on with them before anyone might object. "Your hair is unwashed, despite the lateness of the day, which indicates to me either a lack of interest in your appearance, which I find unlikely, or a harried lifestyle."

Emily softened at that. "You're right. Time is always a concern for me and my responsibilities are many."

Good show, Holmes, I thought. He was displaying empathy, and winning over Emily's trust.

"Your clothes are wrinkled, your collar frayed, the skin of your hands toughened by labor, not at all gentle and soft," Holmes added. "This suggests to me that your priorities are not those of a wife and mother; perhaps you are a widow, and having no child to care for, you exaggerate the importance of your duties to this house in order to—"

"That's quite enough!" Emily cried. "Out! The two of you!"

EDITORS' NOTES: SHOW DON'T TELL

We can just imagine how flabbergasted poor Watson must be at this point. Empathy _is_ all important, particularly when selling to women. Showing, not just telling, that you respect and understand them, taking the time to learn what's important to them and how they want to be treated—that you appreciate how valuable their time is—can work miracles in any scenario.

With car buying, not only can it get you on the road to making a sale, but it can also forge a lifelong relationship that will profit you for many years to come. Holmes is clearly trying, but he's still got a long way to go. Maybe he's caught in the cycle of automatically viewing women as part of the "traditional" family, with a husband who is the breadwinner, a wife who is the homemaker, and 2.3 children to round out the equation.

But in today's world, that demographic only accounts for 13.9% of the population. Fortunately for Holmes, he's got a friend by his side who truly knows the score!   —R&M

Holmes looked stunned and perplexed. He had gone too far in his attempt to dazzle Emily with his astounding skills of observation and deduction. Ultimately he came across as little more than a show-off, a know-it-all, on subjects that were not pertinent to the matter at hand.

"Wait," Holmes said. "We really must—"

"Dash it all, man, you've done quite enough," I said. "Now leave this matter to me."

Holmes withdrew and I spent a good ten minutes simply *listening* to Emily as she vented her justifiable complaints about Holmes' behavior. And listening, as I've come to learn, is more than half the battle....

EDITORS' NOTES: THE TOP 10 THINGS *NOT* TO DO WHEN LISTENING TO A CUSTOMER

You think you're a great listener. You put a lot of time and effort into coming up with ways to make your customer know you're paying attention, really hanging on his or her every word. When you're face-to-face with a customer, your mind is constantly whirling with ideas, information, comebacks and so on. *Yet*...something's not right. The customer comes right out and says you're not listening to her. Or even worse, she doesn't say it, but you can feel the tension in the air. You know things aren't going well. You have to ask yourself, "What's going wrong and how can I fix it?" A good place to start is by avoiding these common listening errors.

1. Avoid planning to talk rather than listening.
2. Don't decide you know what's going on inside the customer's mind and what she's all about.
3. Avoid constantly interrupting the customer, even if it's to agree, ask questions, or give suggestions.
4. Don't try to filter out anything that doesn't apply to you or how you see the subject at hand.
5. Avoid changing the subject or trying to control it.
6. Don't be argumentative, try to prove the customer wrong, or attempt to "pacify" the customer.
7. Avoid making the conversation about you.
8. Don't look at your watch, daydream, think about being anywhere else, or mentally formulate an escape route.
9. Avoid thinking about anything other than the customer's words when she is talking; this includes mentally creating a plan to make yourself seem polite and kind to the customer.

10. Don't try to buy time so that you can come up with a clever comeback instead of listening to and answering direct questions.   —R&M

Finally, with no encouragement from me, Emily shook her head and said, "Truly, I get no feeling of malice from the man. Simply a lack of certain basic skills."

"And without those skills," I said, "I'm sure *you* yourself could hardly do your job as the proprietor of this boarding house."

Emily's face brightened the moment I sincerely conveyed my understanding of her circumstances and viewpoint. "Exactly so," she said.

I then told her what I could of the case Holmes and I were working on, and she quickly gave me a good idea of the esteem with which she held young Mr. Dooley. He was a kind man, quiet, perhaps not entirely sure of his own worth. He was never one to pry, but he was always available when anyone needed to talk.

"Oh, and he's a scribbler, much like the man he works for," she added.

"A fellow writer?" I asked.

"Indeed," she confirmed. "He worships that Wells fellow. Wants to be just like him."

It took very little persuading to coax Emily into allowing us to examine Mr. Dooley's room. She admitted that he had not been to meals for several days and she had been concerned about him even before we appeared.

Holmes wisely did not open his mouth again. He seemed excited enough to have Dooley's room opened and to be once again on the hunt. If only I could have made my friend see that the true locked door in this house was not made of wood, but the iron will of Emily Bradley. That door only opened when plied with a key forged of *sincerity* and *respect*.

Within Dooley's room, we discovered evidence that he had actually moved out of the boarding house—a fact that stunned Emily Bradley. Yet the evidence was irrefutable. His clothes and all his valuables had been packed up and removed. Holmes found an outline of dust around a shape that corresponded perfectly to a common and inexpensive traveling bag, and several other clues to support the conclusion that Mr. Dooley had fled the premises.

Rummaging through some of the trash he had left behind, we found several drafts of a letter addressed to a woman Dooley referred to only as "L." In the letter, he spoke of an opportunity that had recently presented itself, one he did not believe she would approve of, but one that was necessary for him to make his fortune and prove that he was 'marriageable material.'

"I fear Mr. Dooley may have done something fool-ish," Emily said, helping as we overturned every inch of the room. She knew nothing of Dooley's beloved; however, with her aid, we discovered a photograph that had fallen behind a now-empty bookcase. A fiery-haired woman smiled up at us from the black and white picture, which had light colors added by an artist—a common enough practice. Behind the woman in the photo sat our only clue to discovering the woman's whereabouts: One of the most expensive automobiles available today.

When it was time to leave, Holmes took to the street to search for a Hansom while I spoke again to Emily Bradley.

"He truly is of another age, is he not?" she remarked.

"I believe he can be of this one," I said.

"I can understand a desire to cling to that which is familiar and comforting," she said, her fingers absently grazing her wedding band. "But Mr. Holmes pushes away the very aid he most requires!"

Her deductions were entirely correct. When old methods no longer work, or when methods that work with a certain clientele clearly do not work within a new framework, then change must be embraced.

"I wish you both luck," she said.

I had a sense she was referring to more than our case, yet I feared we would need luck—and more than luck—in that regard, as well. Our next stop was an automotive dealer, one of only three in London that sold the expensive automobile before which Dooley's love was standing in the photograph.

I sighed. Holmes refused to even *ride* in a car. How would he react when *surrounded* by them? I would soon find out. That—and many other things…

Chapter Three Checklist

COMPETENCY EXPLORED IN THIS CHAPTER

Establish a Trusting Relationship.
Uncover Her Specific Needs and Wants.
✓ **Make A Professional Sales Presentation.**
Complete a Pressure-less Closing.
Build an Enhanced Relationship with Her and Hers.
Provide Efficient, Non-Intrusive Administration.

COMPETENCIES—*collections of observable behaviors in categories that, when demonstrated, indicate a level of successful performance.*

BEHAVIORS—*each competency is followed by a series of phrases that describe actions (or behaviors) characteristic of a person who performs with a high degree of ability in that area. The behaviors will be demonstrated, in varying degrees, by those with different abilities and positions.*

KEEP IN MIND

✓ Today only 13.9% of the families in America resemble the model of the "traditional family" in which the woman stays at home while the husband works.

THINK

✓ What is the #1 buying criteria for this woman? How can I demonstrate that knowledge?

✓ I walk into each sales situation comfortable in the belief that this customer interaction will have a positive outcome.

SAY
✓ I'd like to explain the options regarding buying or leasing a car.

DO
✓ Demonstrate your ability to take what she has said and recommend a car that will meet her needs.
✓ Focus on promotions that best fit her needs.
✓ Dress like a person of business, not like someone who just walked onto the lot.
✓ *Take pride in your job.* Know your product and your company. Be able to answer any questions about a particular car that a customer might have.
✓ Give her your total attention—tell the receptionist that you are with an important customer and you are not to be disturbed.
✓ Reference the convenience and reliability of your service department and your willingness to stick with her from sale to service and back.
✓ Utilize your sales and marketing materials to inform the customer of the reasons she will be happy buying your product.

✓ *Time is money.* Be aware that her time is precious and that she has many responsibilities. Many women (65 million in the U.S.) work outside the home from 9-5, cook and clean, take the kids to school and pick them up, and then get their husbands to the train station, etc. You might be surprised, once your woman customer has decided what vehicle she wants to buy, how many women would rather cut to the chase and do a deal as quickly as possible. That's good. Good for her, and good for you.

✓ *Listen and learn.* Be willing to listen and let her vent her frustrations if she wants to talk about prior bad treatment that she has experienced when car-buying. She is giving you blow-by-blow instruction in what not to do, so listen carefully!

DON'T

✓ *Condescend.* Don't talk to women with the same "reassuring" tone you would use with children. Women will pick up on this instantly and go on the defensive.

✓ *Dismiss.* Don't ask to speak to "the man in charge" or dismiss a woman customer on her own by asking her to come back "when she's serious."

✓ *Generalize.* Making assumptions about a woman's personality simply because she is a woman is likely to get you in trouble. Not every woman is "nurturing" or "over-sensitive" or "emotional" or any of the labels frequently applied. Every person is different. Treat each customer as an individual. Knowledge is power, so get to know each customer and the basic differences between men and women; then you will have all you need to be successful every time and give yourself the power to make the sale!

✓ Ask in any form: "Are all the decision-makers here?" Considering almost 50% of women are single, you have a high chance of irritating every woman customer. The risk is too high that the question will backfire.

Chapter Four

Dealings with Destiny

The ride to the first of the dealerships was oddly somber. Holmes sat silently in the Hansom, looking out at the bumpy, jittering world and displaying none of the usual excitement that went with running down a clue. "I feel I've been acting quite the fool," Holmes unexpectedly confessed.

"You are many things," I said comfortingly, "a fool is not one of them. You're one of the least foolish men I've ever had the pleasure to know."

"Yet I am adrift. In the early days of our adventures, I would *never* have made a blunder such as the one I made with the widow Bradley. So much of our world has changed. Up is down and down is up. A *woman* letting out rooms to make ends meet? Naturally. Yet so many other constants in my mind have turned out to no longer be valid that I decided this one must not be so. And as to my insults to her vanity…I *tried* to treat her as I might a man. That would *seem* to be the logical way to proceed in this new and far more equal setting. Yet this too backfired on me."

"Watson, in what regard have I failed?" Holmes asked. "Treat men and women differently and there is trouble. Treat them the same and there is equal trouble."

"Not at all," I said. "The trick, if I can call it that, is understanding when to treat men and women differently, and when to treat them the same."

EDITORS' NOTES: WHAT WOMEN WANT
According to our studies, women are far more likely to respond positively to environments in which they are *not* treated exactly the same as men. The same amount of respect and consideration, yes, but in a selling or service environment, dealerships that take the particular needs and interests of women into consideration sell more cars to women and keep more women as loyal customers and vocals advocates. How can you tell what women want?
***Ask* them. You won't regret it. Now—back to the great detective (though we're starting to wonder if it's Holmes or *Watson* who deserves that title)!   —R&M**

I waited until Holmes looked my way before I continued. Once I had his gaze, I held it, unwaveringly, with mine. "I always find it best to treat women with the same amount of respect that I would care to be treated."

"I certainly have no desire to treat a man or woman any other way," Holmes said.

"That's easy enough to say, but much harder to do."

"What do you mean?" Holmes asked.

"Even when you have the best of intentions, you can easily make an error simply because women are socialized differently than men. For example, you might use the exact same turns of phrase on your male and female clients. You might even use the same gestures and behaviors, yet the men will interpret these phrases and gestures differently than the women, simply because men and women are brought up differently." Holmes looked away, so I refrained from further conversation. Several long moments passed before Holmes turned back and fixed me with his piercing gaze once more.

"Why did you stop talking?" he asked. "The silence was utterly distressing."

"Distressing to *you*," I said.

"What are you on about, Watson?"

"I was teaching you a lesson, my friend. When you fail to *look* at a woman when she's speaking, she will quite often decide it is because you are *not paying any attention* to her words."

"But I was simply considering your statements!"

"That's not how a *woman* might take it," I said. "Do you recall my conversation with Emily Bradley?"

"I do," he said dourly. "And I will admit, it went a shade better than my talk with her."

"As I spoke, you may have noticed that she was *nodding her head*. Holmes, what do you think that indicates? A woman's nodding of her head?"

"That she was *agreeing* with you, of course!"

"No. When a *man* does that, it means he agrees. A woman is simply letting you know that she's *listening*."

"Hmph," Holmes said as we pulled up to a busy intersection. "So there is a complex methodology to all of this."

"I'd say there are certain guidelines to follow, a method of a kind…but really more of a reorienting how one views—"

Holmes briskly waved his hand. "I must lead with my strengths in this. Methodology is the cornerstone of my existence, Watson. I now feel that I have hope in this endeavor!"

The driver called out that we had arrived, minutes later, we were on the first of the three lots. A salesperson immediately approached us. His energy and enthusiasm were high, until he learned we hadn't actually come to make a purchase. This was disappointing to me, and seemed shortsighted. My wife and I had been talking about purchasing an automobile. Had this man been more pleasant and interested, even though a sale was not in the offing this day, I might have considered coming back to him in the future.

Having learned our lesson at the first dealership, Holmes and I proceeded to the second. In this case we did pretend to be interested in the purchase of an automobile, and Holmes gave an admirable performance as a potential buyer, his true feelings about the "contraptions" buried so deeply even I, who had been privy to his earlier rants, would never have guessed them.  Unfortunately, the salesperson we spoke with, and his superior, had no recollection of the young lady in the photograph, who we maintained was the new lady in the life of an acquaintance whose address we had misplaced. If we could speak with her, she could put us in touch with our friend.

Our tactics may have been sharper, but the end result was the same at the third and last dealership: no one knew her. We were about to leave, dejected and without further direction, when Holmes pointed glee-fully at a particular car in the service department.

"That's it!" he exclaimed. "That is her automobile!"

I shook my head. "It may be the correct make and model, but these machines are mass-produced."

Holmes withdrew the photograph and pointed to a minuscule detail that had escaped my eye: A shiny splinter made of crystal dangling from the rear view mirror. The car in this lot sported the same artifact.

"She may be here right this minute," Holmes said, grasping my arm and leading me to the desk of the service representative, a kindly man named Fetch.

"Do I know her?" he asked, looking at the photo-graph. "Indeed I do. Now *that's* a woman who knows what she wants and won't put up with no shenanigans!"

"Could you tell us where to find her?" I inquired eagerly.

"Could I? Indeed, I could," Fetch said. "Will I, now? I think not. And don't think about loitering about, waiting for her to arrive and claim her car, as she turned it in for another one just this morning. Now good day."

"My good fellow, what's the problem?" Holmes asked.

Fetch smiled. "In my business, we have to think long-term. We're trying to build life-long relationships. That can be difficult, but the rewards make it well worth the effort. How would *you* feel if I passed along information about you to some shady-looking, quick-talking characters who showed up out of the blue? No, sir, old Fetch may be a lot of things, but untrustworthy, loose-lipped, and disrespectful he ain't!"

EDITORS' NOTES: DO THE MATH

We have to take our hats off to Fetch at this point. He understands that if you want to be a top salesperson then you have to cultivate repeat buyers/long-term customers. How you treat them today in large part determines how much money you make in the future and how hard you have to work at those sales. Another way to say this is that retention of a known customer is much easier than the acquisition of a new one. Too often we are short-sighted about the value of a customer. We opt to make a couple of bucks today and forego thousands of dollars in the future. Let's get specific and talk numbers so you can set up your own goal and measure your progress against that goal.

A ten car per month salesperson is considered average, while twenty is excellent, and thirty a franchise player. If you aspire to be a franchise player (and why wouldn't you?) you need to sell to 40% of your customers each month, so

that means you have to be in front of 120 customers a month in order to sell 30 cars. Do that every month for a year and you would have sold 360 cars. That also means that you have established meaningful relationships with these buyers so that when they decide to purchase another car in four years (the average amount of time buyers keep their vehicles) they will not consider buying from anyone else.

So, to calculate the total number of meaningful, repeat buyers you need to develop to become a franchise player with 30 cars per month consistently, multiply 360 relationships/buyers by four years. That will give you 1,440 relationships with individuals that trust you most and wouldn't even think of buying a car before contacting you. That's the goal—and the way to get rich selling cars!

—R&M

By this time, several customers had lined up behind us, and a look between Holmes and myself signaled our agreement that Fetch would not be forthcoming. We stepped out of line, found a nearby bench, and sat down. It had been a trying day.

A pair of salespeople passed us.

"But where are we going to find someone who specializes in selling to women?" the closest man asked.

"I have no idea. I was simply told to find someone, and to do so as soon as humanly possible!"

They drifted into the main building of the dealership and Holmes jumped to his feet.

"That's it, Watson! I shall apply for that position. With the insights you have given me, I am bound to become an instant success!"

I said nothing. I wanted to believe Holmes was joking, but I knew from his tone that he was not. There was so much about selling to women that he had yet to learn.

"You don't even know how to *drive* an automobile!" I told him.

"Wells is bound to have one of these contraptions," Holmes said. "Have him bring it and the driver's manual over to 221B post-haste. I shall learn all I need to know, acquire this position, and use it to gain access to the dealership's records. Then we will find our mystery woman!"

I spent the better part of an hour attempting to talk Holmes out of his scheme, but in the end I relented. There were other avenues of investigation I wished to pursue in this case, and I would busy myself with them until Holmes returned.

Little did I know the astonishing news my friend would soon bring me, and the impact it would have on this case.

Chapter Four Checklist

COMPETENCY EXPLORED IN THIS CHAPTER

Establish a Trusting Relationship.
Uncover Her Specific Needs and Wants.
Make A Professional Sales Presentation.
✓ **Complete a Pressure-less Closing.**
Build an Enhanced Relationship with Her and Hers.
Provide Efficient, Non-Intrusive Administration.

COMPETENCIES—*collections of observable behaviors in categories that, when demonstrated, indicate a level of successful performance.*

BEHAVIORS—*each competency is followed by a series of phrases that describe actions (or behaviors) characteristic of a person who performs with a high degree of ability in that area. The behaviors will be demonstrated, in varying degrees, by those with different abilities and positions.*

THINK

✓ Women sometimes need time to consider all the information they have been given. I should offer her a place where she can review if necessary.

✓ She will give me all the information I need to close the deal *if* I *listen* to what she is saying and give her what she wants.

✓ *Understanding gives me the edge.* Sometimes a woman wants to be treated the same as a man, but most times she wants to be treated differently. It all comes down to my understanding the pressures women face that men often do not have to worry about, as well as the interests women have that men often don't relate to. When I am unsure how to treat a woman, I should ask her. I should always treat women with the same respect with which I would want to be treated and the same respect with which I would treat any woman who is important to me.

✓ *Different signals.* I should recognize that when a woman nods her head, it means she is *listening* to me, *not* that she is *agreeing* with me. I should always *look* at a woman when she is talking to me, otherwise she will think I am *not listening.*

SAY
✓ What do you need to make your decision?
✓ How can I follow-up with you later? Would you prefer a phone call, a fax, or an e-mail?
✓ Have I answered all your questions?

DO

✓ Provide her with all the information she needs to make an informed decision.

✓ Keep your promises.

✓ Act as intermediary with the finance department to ensure that the customer understands and agrees to the total cost of the deal.

✓ Show her any practical items in the car that would help her be more efficient. (But don't give her lessons in automotive engineering).

✓ Have a list of satisfied customers who bought the same car that she can contact.

✓ Once she has decided to buy a car, move the sales process along as speedily as possible so that you don't waste her time.

✓ Surprise her by doing the unexpected. For example, keep a tab at a nearby restaurant and suggest that she go there (either alone or with whoever she brought with her) for lunch after she has decided to purchase a car while her paperwork is being drawn up.

DON'T

✓ *Lose your enthusiasm.* Don't let your enthusiasm for a customer's business diminish if she decides not to buy a car today. Treat her well and she will remember you (and recommend you to her friends) when she is ready to buy a car.

✓ Pressure her in any way. Don't play games. The #1 reason that women don't buy from a salesperson is pressure. Move towards closure without making her feel like you are applying pressure. Don't underestimate how much discomfiture can result from a woman feeling pressured. For example, being accosted by a salesperson the moment she steps out of her car will have a woman jumping back into her car and driving away.

Chapter Five

News From the Front

"ood heavens, Holmes!" I cried as I took in the sight of my friend sitting by the window three days later. He looked haggard and forlorn. His eyes were like those I had seen only one other time in my life, and I said as much. "You look like you've been through war!"

"I feel it, too," Holmes said weakly.

"Things did not go well, I take it," I said, sitting beside him.

"The job was mine," Holmes said, drifting off for a moment into a rare state of befuddlement before snapping back to attention at the jarring sound of an automobile's blaring horn. I leaned over and closed the window.

"Incredible," I whispered.

He shook his head. "It was the intelligence you gathered that won the day, Watson. I found it easy enough to play the part initially, at least during the interview. It wasn't until they shuffled me out onto the floor and straight at my first woman customer that the harsh reality of it all struck me. People are complex creatures. Women and men. Yet the differences between the two can be staggering!"

"There are differences, yes," I said, "but given a certain openness to new ideas and points of view, those differences can be something to celebrate."

"So you say," Holmes whispered. "And for many a merry gent, I'm sure that is true. On this day, I cannot number myself among them."

"What happened?"

"I applied scientific method. Deduction. Reason. Each encounter should have proven successful. Instead…disaster."

"I'm sure it wasn't that bad."

"Agreed. I'd wager that I'm indulging in what that Freud fellow we saw at the club would call 'blocking.' Yes, Watson, it was probably far, far worse. But I will give you what details I can."

Holmes told me of Winifred Manifold, his first customer. He blinded me with details about her precise manner of dress, the way she carried herself, the style of her hair, the complexion of her skin. I soon felt as though I might go mad if I heard any more pointless description. Did he honestly believe the precise number of eyelashes she possessed made any kind of difference in the type of person she was, or what technique would be needed to sell her a car?

Horrifyingly, he did.

"Scientific method, Watson. When a woman bats her eyelashes, it may signal a great many things. Thus the number of eyelashes a woman possesses takes on a great significance. A woman with fewer eyelashes, for example, is bound to feel inferior to one with an abundance, because her tools for signifying just how shy she is, how wilting, the manner in which she prefers to be 'courted,' if you will—"

"Holmes, you were there to sell automobiles, not make dates!"

"Naturally, but can *she* know that? I think not."

"Of course," I said. "That is why any woman would enter a dealership. She wishes to find the man of her dreams and be swept off her feet. The petty bother of actually purchasing a vehicle *must* be a secondary consideration."

Holmes clutched his head. "It all made such sense at the time. Fetch me a brandy, will you?"

"Are you certain you have not been indulging already?"

"I have not."

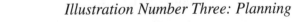

Illustration Number Three: Planning
Holmes has decided to change, and has dedicated himself to
creating a plan. He's about to find out that not just any plan
will do. If only he'd listened to Watson, his plan would have
been very different. At least he's trying!

I rose and returned quickly with a drink. He downed it at once, his face flushing. Then his countenance grew pale once more. Holmes returned to the dissertation of his methodology.

"Foreheads, it seemed to me, were highly important. A high forehead, particularly one that protrudes, would indicate a slow thinker—"

"I do think you've gone mad."

"But there is a logic to it! For example, if a woman is of the larger variety, taking a dress size, let us say, several times above the norm, then her personality would be just as sizable."

"A sunny complexion equals a sunny disposition," I muttered.

"Yes, yes, exactly so!"

"You worked all this out on your own?"

"It's entirely your fault."

"Mine?" I cried. "Holmes, how can this be *my* fault, even in the slightest? I tried to warn you that—"

"You told me to try to imagine what life must be like for a woman in today's society, and that is what I did. I even spoke to each of them *as if* I were enjoying the conversation."

"Did it ever occur to you that if you allowed yourself the pleasure, then talking to women, even during the sales process, might indeed *be* a pleasure?"

EDITORS' NOTES: COMMUNICATION IS KEY

You know what you're trying to communicate, but for some reason the customer seems to be getting a completely different message. If this keeps up, you might lose the sale. Why is this happening? What can you do about it?

Consider this: When you are talking with a customer, remember that communication consists of three parts: *content*, *delivery*, and *situation*. The effects of any of the three can be destroyed or magnified by the other two. You must make sure that your content and delivery are appropriate for the situation and are in agreement. If you feel that you are not being understood properly by the customer, ask yourself these simple questions:

✓ Is it *what* I'm saying?
✓ Is it *how* I'm saying it?
✓ Is it the *situation* itself?

Too bad poor Sherlock didn't know this before he went to the dealership!   —R&M

"I tried to consider each woman in terms of her physical frailties," Holmes continued. "Many women shrink from a loud voice, as you must know."

"REALLY?" I bellowed, causing Holmes to recoil. I smiled. "Well, so long as we're clear it's only women!"

"I even offered to help Winifred's son with his homework."

"Was this *before* or *after* the fascinating introduction of her heavy purse to your forehead?" I asked, only now spotting the bruise on the far side of his skull, which had been hidden from view by the deep shadows cast by the morning light.

"That was not Winifred. That was Mrs. Tanner, the delightful woman whose well-placed blow helped me out of that wretched situation."

"You mean, you were fired?"

"For matters of personal conduct. And for not selling a single car. That latter point was entirely the fault of my methodology. It had nothing to do with the buying power of the clientele—you were right about that, Watson. After all, why would the dealership have a position for selling to women if such sales were impossible to make, or if women did not have buying power? Yet there was one salesperson who was a naysayer all along. He called any woman who walked into the dealership a 'one-legger.'"

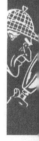

"Indeed. Why so?"

"According to him, a woman on her own was merely one half of a decision-making unit. It instantly followed, for him at least, that a woman could not make a decision without consulting and gaining the permission and financial support of a husband or beau. He would often tell women to turn around and come back when they were properly accompanied by a male. Needless to say, none of them ever came back."

"Beastly."

"Yes, but not far removed from my behavior with Emily Bradley, I'm sorry to say. At least I can justify my motives as being pure, though motive hardly negates the end result of driving away one with whom you wish to do business. The true bottom line here is that I never lost a sale because I believed I was wasting my time. So I must be learning something through all of this."

"I believe you are, Holmes."

"Yesterday, two women entered the dealership independent of one another. I could only attend the needs of one, and the selfsame salesperson who I mentioned a moment earlier was forced to attend the other. She was very young, but clearly well off. She selected the most expensive and stylish red sports car on the lot and told the salesperson flat out that she had the buying power to purchase it and was ready to make a deal. The salesperson convinced her to take the car to her beau and let him see it before making a decision, and he did so because he didn't credit her with possessing the power she claimed to have.

"While she was gone, he called about and made inquiries, quickly learning that she was representing herself honestly. But when she returned, she handed him the keys and said the deal was off. Her beau took one look at the car and became jealous and upset over the idea that she would be driving a motorcar that was so far superior in looks and performance to his own.

"She said that if she had already made the purchase, she would have put in the time and effort to quell his objections. But because she hadn't, she instead decided it wasn't worth the trouble. The salesperson had chased his sale right out the door simply because of his pre-conceptions!

"Then there is the matter of who to address if a man and a woman enter the dealership together," Holmes continued. "The mystery can be solved with a few simple questions, and by allowing the primary driver of the vehicle to identify her or himself, as they invariably will. But the salesperson who was so closed to selling to women *always* spoke to the man, ignoring the woman—even a woman who explained that the man with her was only a friend and not the primary decision maker, nor the person with the power to make the purchase."

"Good heavens, Holmes, my spirits are lifting to hear you make such observations."

"Worst of all are the high pressure tactics," said Holmes. "I saw that salesperson bring a woman into a room and badger her over why she was not buying. He cited the three 'M's, demanding to know if she was not buying because of the 'Money,' the 'Machine,' or 'Me.' The customer left immediately. And all the back and forth, running to the manager for every little question, did nothing but erode the customer's confidence."

"Indeed," I said, delighted by the unexpected outpouring of good old-fashioned common sense wisdom my friend was sharing.

"I was not the only salesperson to have found difficulties in this task, though I hardly agree with the reasons they gave. Many others said that women were difficult. They claimed that women took much more time and couldn't come to a decision. *Balderdash!* At least with women there was no game-playing, no massaging of egos or assuming subservient roles so as not to engage in battles over alpha-wolf pack superiority, as there was with the male customers I saw.

"Men were far more prone to buy automobiles based on emotion, whereas women considered practicality and the golden rule of form follows function as their primary concern. Women were also more articulate and open to receiving mentoring in areas where they had not or could not research in advance."

EDITORS' NOTES: BE THE COACH

When a woman asks a salesperson a direct question about gas mileage and safety ratings, and is instead diverted to issues such as the color of a car or other superficial matters, sales are often driven right off the lot! A woman wants to be guided and informed, not sold. She wants her questions answered.

The satisfying quality of the encounter and the promise of forging a lifelong relationship best appeals to women car buyers, making them willing to spend more or travel greater distances to gain the assurance that their "car guy or gal" will be there for them when needed. A good experience will also get them talking to all their friends, recommending certain salespeople for more business. One sale isn't necessarily just one sale with women customers, the numbers can expand exponentially!   —R&M

I settled back and sighed.

Holmes had gained many insights, and his intentions were pure, but he still believed in applying a single uniform scientific methodology to women based on outward characteristics instead of data derived from open-ended questioning and proper listening.

At least Holmes was open to change. That much was clear from what he said he'd learned watching the salespeople at work. And he was willing to learn even more. Yet I despaired over the sad condition his travails had left him.

"This is, in part, my fault," I conceded. "I should have applied for the job instead. I knew from the start that you were not the person to put in—"

Holmes waved a rolled up paper before me.

"What's this," I asked.

"That is precisely the information I went to the dealership to ascertain," Holmes said.

I examined the papers. They were copies scrawled in Holmes' distinctive style. The first listed the contact information for a certain Lysette Price, the woman in the photograph we'd found in Dooley's room. The second was some kind of itinerary. Trafalgar Square at ten this morning was circled.

"It's where she will be," Holmes said.

"Tell me this information was not derived through your *unusual* new methodology."

"No," Holmes said, slapping his hands on his knees and rising with a spring in his step I hardly expected to see. "For this, I led with my strengths and went with what I knew. If you doubt me, Watson, you don't have to come. I simply thought you might wish to be present when I confront this young woman and reveal her role in these dark dealings."

"Her role? Isn't that deduction a tad premature?"

"Not at all, Watson," Holmes said, gathering his coat and hat. "And when I share with you what I've learned, you too will arrive at the conclusion that she is an accomplice to the young Mr. Dooley's schemes."

"I suppose I *should* come," I said, following him to the door with the tread of a disappointed man.

Indeed, Holmes' had accomplished the task of ferreting out the precise information he'd needed. He'd learned the name of Lysette Price. Yet I had wanted him to learn much more. I had wanted him to gain the skills necessary to help him adjust to our new and ever-changing world, particularly in understanding and coping with the role *women* now played in every aspect of society and commerce. Only with those skills could he possibly hope to thrive in the field he so loved.

Holmes grinned. "Come, Watson. Mastering the craft needed to fully appreciate and communicate with women may still elude me, but a *criminal* mind—male or female—is one I will have no trouble fathoming!"

Perhaps Holmes was right. I can never know. But Lysette Price was no criminal. Her true part in all of this was far more complicated. In fact, it was tied so tightly with the business of automobiles and women that it soon made me consider whether or not she inspired the very vision of the future found in the missing manuscript that had prompted Wells to visit us in the first place.

Only a firm mastery of the very skills Holmes was now eschewing would reveal the answers. Thus my work in this business was just beginning.

Chapter Five Checklist

COMPETENCY EXPLORED IN THIS CHAPTER

Establish a Trusting Relationship.
Uncover Her Specific Needs and Wants.
Make A Professional Sales Presentation.
Complete a Pressure-less Closing.
✓ **Build an Enhanced Relationship with Her and Hers.**
Provide Efficient, Non-Intrusive Administration.

COMPETENCIES—*collections of observable behaviors in categories that, when demonstrated, indicate a level of successful performance.*

BEHAVIORS—*each competency is followed by a series of phrases that describe actions (or behaviors) characteristic of a person who performs with a high degree of ability in that area. The behaviors will be demonstrated, in varying degrees, by those with different abilities and positions.*

KEEP IN MIND

✓ *What they buy and why.* Remember that men are far more prone to buy cars based on emotion, whereas women put their stock in the golden rule of form follows function.

✓ *Who is actually looking to learn.* Women are more articulate and open to receiving mentoring in areas they are not familiar with. They ask questions.

THINK

✓ The key to relationship building with women is to remember that women talk and the woman customer I make happy today will tell all her friends who are looking for a car about me and my *great* service.

✓ I will benefit from rehearsing with a woman friend or family member how to have a conversation with women.

✓ *Communication is key.* I should consider what I'm saying, how I'm saying it, and the situation my customer is facing. By making adjustments in these three key areas, I have the power to make a real difference in the sales process and win a customer for life.

✓ The best way to build a relationship with a woman customer is to always go above and beyond her expectations, and add value to my service. For example, if she is bringing in her car to be serviced, I should have it washed and vacuumed so she picks up a nice, clean car.

SAY

✓ Would you mind taking some of my business cards to give to anyone you know who is looking for a car?

✓ Do you prefer that I keep in contact by phone or by e-mail?

DO

✓ After the woman buys a car, leave a friendly message on her answering machine: "I am here to help if you need anything. If you have any questions or problems please call me."

✓ Read magazines and newsletters that deal with women's issues so that you can increase your understanding of the things women are interested in, what they are talking about, and what they are feeling. It's also a great way to spot new opportunities.

✓ Contact the customer on a regular basis to evaluate her satisfaction with her purchase.

✓ Facilitate interactions with the service department for the customer.

✓ Monitor service activity of the customer on an ongoing basis to deal with problems that may have arisen with the vehicle.

✓ Find things of value to offer your customer throughout the year and the trade-in cycle.

DON'T

✓ *Mix business with pleasure.* Don't try to make a date with a woman customer. Don't try to impress her by offering to help her children with their homework. Your place is as her salesperson. Try to cross the line and you will lose the sale.

✓ *Invade her space.* Women appreciate being given space. Be available when she needs you, but don't hover or crowd her, and don't box her in.

Chapter Six

The Woman Strikes

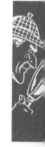

W e had gotten no further than the curb when we were accosted by a familiar fellow. "Holmes!" H.G. Wells hollered. "I want a word with you."

I tensed, worried not only about the delay, but also the effect of our client's temper on Holmes. Wells' face was beet red, his shoulders practically up around his ears.

"I come out this morning and my car has reappeared, but you are nowhere to be seen," Wells said. "I came to you for help and I have no idea what's going on!"

"You're absolutely correct," Holmes said calmly. "I've been terribly remiss in keeping you updated on our progress. There's no excuse for such a thing and I hope you will accept my sincere apologies."

Holmes went on to give Wells a brief summary of what he had discovered. I noted that Holmes made a special effort to keep his hands in view, his thumbs prominent. Additionally, the great detective seemed extremely conscious of Wells' body language.

EDITORS' NOTES: THUMBS UP!

Sometimes it's the little things that make all the difference. A friend of ours in the auto service trade was giving talks to large groups, but he could tell that he wasn't gaining the full trust and attention of his audience. Why?

A professional speaker taught him that it had a lot to do with his thumbs. People always need to see your thumbs when you talk. If they don't, they think that you are untrustworthy, you must be "hiding" something. Crossing your arms over your chest not only indicates defensiveness, it hides your thumbs. If your customers can see your thumbs, they can also see that you're trustworthy.   —R&M

Wells calmed considerably, and even though he wished to come along to interview Lysette Price, Holmes talked him out of it. Instead, Holmes promised to messenger over twice daily updates, and then he asked Wells if his car was running smoothly. It turned out the detective had taken Wells' car in for service while he was working at the dealership and Holmes had even made sure it was washed and waxed. Wells had noticed the latter, and had appreciated the unexpected courtesy, but he hadn't put two and two together to link his car's increased performance with the time it had spent in Holmes' care.

I was impressed, and I said as much as we watched Wells walk down the street to his parked car, looking relaxed and satisfied.

Later, Holmes explained that he had spent a good deal of time with the serviceman Fetch, whose lessons had been quite helpful.

As we waited for a cab, Holmes spoke. "Fetch suggested that one should approach service with the intent to make the customer's day better. He taught me the lesson of 'for good measure.' Simply put, give the customer a little extra and you'll win him or her over every time."

EDITORS' NOTES: SERVICE IS SALES

Now here's a side of Holmes we didn't expect, but it's good to remember that service is sales.

Holmes owned his mistakes, and made it clear that he will honor his promises, doing *what* he said he would do *when* he said he would do it— plus a little more for good measure. Remember, this tactic can only help you when it comes down to those all-important C.S.I. reports. High marks on the Customer Service Index are worth their weight in gold!   —R&M

Even with all the activity in Trafalgar Square, Lysette Price was easy to spot. She stood beside another new model automobile, this one designed for families. Her blazing red hair was aglow with bright sunlight and her smile was warmer still.

Holmes walked briskly in her direction, his gaze narrow, his purpose set. I felt an instant sense of foreboding.

"Now, Holmes, remember all you've learned," I said.

"Watson, through the years I have learned much about the criminal mind, and one thing of which I remain certain is that the hand of justice must be firm. Criminals must see that there is no way out of their predicament. Only a full and speedy confession may lessen their punishment."

"You don't *know* that Miss Price is a criminal, or even an accomplice to whatever Dooley is planning."

"But I do. It is the only logical conclusion. Look at her—all smiles and glee. She is putting on an act, my good man, attempting to deflect suspicion by carrying on as if everything were normal. And that, under these highly unusual circumstances, is of itself completely damning."

Before I could object further, Holmes was upon Lysette Price, raising his walking stick and demanding her undivided attention. The woman with whom Lysette had been chatting dashed off.

Holmes had explained that Lysette's job was to drive about London and strike up conversations with women in hopes of interesting them in the vehicles sold by the dealership for which both she and Holmes worked. She looked none-too-pleased that her prospect had been run off in such a fashion.

Her warmth turned to ice as she took in Holmes and said, "Well, if it isn't the inglorious Mr. Rollo Peppers."

I couldn't help but smirk upon hearing that ridiculous name. Holmes said he had assumed a false identity and disguise for his brief tenure as a car salesman, but...Rollo Peppers?

"Really, Holmes," I muttered.

The detective cleared his throat. "Why do you address me that way?"

Illustration Number Four: Executing
*Seriously, would you buy a car from this man? Didn't think so. Holmes has put his plan into motion and transformed himself into the soon-to-be infamous Rollo Peppers. This is **executing,** the trial and error stage of making a lasting change. Hang in there, Sherlock! Big things are heading your way, including many changes for the better.*

"Oh, come now," Lysette said. "Don't you think I *saw* you at the dealership?"

It was Holmes' turn to be taken by surprise. "But...I did not see you!"

"Such was my desire. You made such a botch of things, insulted and drove away so many women with your behavior, I had—and still have—no interest in dealing with you."

Holmes shook his head. "I was wearing a disguise."

"Yes, *that* I could ascertain even at a distance. My parents were in the theater, as they say. The position I hold now is only to keep me until I find more steady employment in the motion picture arena. The stage is not my calling. But all this is far more than you have any right to know about me, particularly as your disgraceful performance nearly cost me my job!"

"But... but...Now see here," Holmes sputtered.

I sighed. This interview had gotten off on the wrong foot from the first moment of contact, and I feared there would be no recalling it from the brink.

"Who do you think got those women interested in visiting the dealership in the first place?" Lysette continued, sticking one gloved finger in Holmes' wide-eyed and mystified face. "*Me*, that's who. You don't have to be Sherlock bloody Holmes to figure that one out!"

"But I *am* Sherlock bloody Holmes!" he cried.

She hesitated and smiled. "I suspected as much. Thank you for confirming it."

Holmes shoulders fell. He had been undone.

EDITORS' NOTES: BE LIKE COLUMBO

While we're on the topic of some of our favorite detectives, we'd like to mention one who really gets it right: Lt. Columbo. Consider his major "selling points" and see if you can make them work for you!

Lt. Columbo is...

>   **Unthreatening (and unthreatened)**
>   **Humble**
>   **Complimentary**
>   **No ego-involved**
>   **Focus on the end result**
>   **Curious**
>   **Respectful**
>   **Kind**
>   **Successful**

It's too bad the good lieutenant can't sit down with Holmes and teach him a thing or two. Fortunately, Watson's doing a great job whipping him into shape.   —R&M

"Now what do you want with me?" Lysette asked. "I've done nothing wrong, nor do I have knowledge of any crime. And by the way, you are wrinkled, rumpled, and altogether unpresentable. Your appearance hardly elicits the formidable sense of authority you clearly wish to project, considering your tone and manner, let alone making me wish to be seen with you in public."

Then she turned to me. Her gaze softened a little as she said, "And you must be Dr. John Watson. I've truly enjoyed your accounts of Mr. Holmes' exploits. Now that I've met the man in person, my esteem only rises. It seems you are an excellent *fiction* writer, not merely a biographer as I had thought."

"Lysette," I started, then halted. "*May* I call you Lysette?"

She nodded sharply.

"May I offer my apologies for the manner in which you were approached, and ask for another chance to discuss a very important matter with you?"

"You may *ask*," she said. "Provided you keep your queries within the context of polite conversation, you may ask anything you wish. That doesn't mean I will be moved to answer you, considering the conversation thus far."

I did not look away from her intense green eyes. "That is more than generous," I replied.

Beside me, Holmes still looked as if he was trying to work out what had gone wrong. I could tell him easily, but there was more important work to be done.

I had to impress upon Lysette Price the seriousness of our mission, and I had to do so immediately.

EDITORS' NOTES: KNOCK OFF THE CHIP

Wow—Lysette certainly is going to be one tough egg to crack! She reminds us of so many women customers who enter car dealerships with chips on their shoulders, very heavy baggage from previous unpleasant car-buying experiences.

The best way to approach a woman entering any sales situation is to assume nothing. Display a warm smile, a strong handshake, and a way of walking and holding yourself that suggests an air of humility and genuine desire to be of assistance. In other words, do not display a hint of a swagger, trace of a smirk, or any other expression that might trigger a defensive response. This is the best way to approach *any* situation with women.

Also, if you have trouble remembering someone's name, take out a notepad and ask permission to write it down, along with other per-

tinent details. This lets the customer know that she is your top priority and that you are making a conscious effort to pay her every respect possible. No one appreciates having vital information forgotten in a sales scenario. Try to work on your customer approach at home (along with strong listening techniques). Practice in front of mirrors, and with family, friends, loved ones, and see if it doesn't strengthen all your relationships.

Think like a doctor, and let the first rule be *Do No Harm*. Your patients—we mean *customers*— will thank you for it.   —R&M

I stepped forward, so that I would not have to shout over the noise of the crowd in Trafalgar Square. "Lysette, this concerns your beau, Jonathan Dooley. Are you aware that he has been missing for several days?"

Her expression changed. I saw a flicker of surprise, then a deep sorrow. "I cannot help you."

"Mr. Dooley did not disappear alone," Holmes said, regaining his bearings. His tone was as menacingly matter-of-fact as I have ever heard it.

She shrugged. "What he does, and who he does it with, is no concern of mine. Not any longer."

"Not a *who*, but a *what*," I said, not wishing to lead her astray with innuendo. "He left Mr. Wells' employ with no notice at the exact same time a manuscript he was preparing for Wells vanished. There is an unfortunate, but inescapable connection."

"So your priority is to help Wells," she said, her ire rising once again.

"Our desire is to promote justice," Holmes said.

"That certainly wasn't on your mind at the dealership," she said, whirling on the detective. "Was it justice for women to arrive expecting 'expert assistance' on a matter that is serious to them only to have their hopes dashed by your cold and arrogant treatment of them. None of us wishes to be condescended to, or dealt with as if we were not highly intelligent individual. And all because you had some other agenda in your head."

Holmes was silent. Lysette was correct, of course. Yet I couldn't let the challenge go unanswered.

"Lysette, I must point out to you that my friend Holmes' methods may have been misguided, but they were not driven by carelessness or malice. His desire to fulfill his function at that dealership was genuine—"

"Watson, you mustn't," Holmes tried to interrupt, but I continued.

"Further," I added, "I believe you know far more about this matter than you let on. Consider, please, that a man's reputation is at stake."

A wave of laughter broke over her face. "But which man? And why should I care about that stuffed shirt Wells? Why should I believe *him* above thievery? Would you have me do so because of his station in life? Jonathan slaved for that man, and Wells only notices him now, when things are amiss. I dare say that if his precious manuscript had not disappeared, Wells would have been unlikely to have given Jonathan's state even a shred of concern. And the same, I might venture, would be true of you."

"You still care for him," Holmes said, penetrating her veil of disinterest.

"That is my concern," she said, slightly shaken.

"Finding Jonathan might help clear him of suspicion," I said. "At very least, it would set your mind at ease that he is well."

She turned from us then, retiring to her automobile. "No, I'm sorry. I cannot help you."

"Wait," Holmes called, catching up with her as she turned the key in the ignition. "Let me have one final word with you."

"I am resolute."

"I understand that, and I respect your wishes. But you deserve an apology. I was wrong to treat you as I did. I no longer believe you had anything to do with whatever Mr. Dooley was planning."

"That," she said with a sigh, "is all too true."

EDITORS' NOTES: TREAT HER RIGHT

You just never know. The next customer to enter your showroom or service center may turn out to be the best customer you've ever had, the one who will recommend you to dozens of others, who will make you a "superstar" among your peers. Or maybe not. How can you tell? You can't.

The only way to cover your bases is to treat each customer as if she were a long lost relative who has come to tell you that if you treat her right, you stand to inherit a fortune. Develop the attitude that every customer is valuable and important and you are certain to quickly create an atmosphere of mutual trust and respect—exactly what you need to make that next sale!

—R&M

Lysette Price drove off, and I walked with Holmes in silence. There was little else we could do unless Lysette chose to seek us out and volunteer whatever information she had chosen to withhold. Oh, we might find some pretense to have ourselves let into her dwelling, or learn about her friends to see if one of them was loose-lipped about a confidence. But Holmes and I had silently agreed that to do so in this instance would be wrong. Lysette's comments about the women Holmes had attempted to serve at the dealership had cut deeply, and the detective would not intrude further upon this woman's life unless an invitation was tendered—a likelihood that now seemed remote at best.

Suddenly, Lysette's car pulled up alongside us.

"Get in, Mr. Holmes. Your friend, too. I have a proposal that just might interest you."

Chapter Six
Checklist

COMPETENCY EXPLORED IN THIS CHAPTER

Establish a Trusting Relationship.
Uncover Her Specific Needs and Wants.
Make A Professional Sales Presentation.
Complete a Pressure-less Closing.
Build an Enhanced Relationship with Her and Hers.
✓ Provide Efficient, Non-Intrusive Administration.

COMPETENCIES—*collections of observable behaviors in categories that, when demonstrated, indicate a level of successful performance.*

BEHAVIORS—*each competency is followed by a series of phrases that describe actions (or behaviors) characteristic of a person who performs with a high degree of ability in that area. The behaviors will be demonstrated, in varying degrees, by those with different abilities and positions.*

KEEP IN MIND

✓ According to some data, 85% of medical malpractice cases are based on communication issues. It makes sense that this figure translates roughly to the same percentage of lost sales a salesperson might experience—and for the same basic reason.

✓ **People intuitively sense when someone is distracted. Give your full attention to the matter at hand.**

THINK

✓ **I should be there for the customer when I say I am going to be.**

✓ **I must remember that service does not end after the sale has been made.**

✓ **I will consider the special problems a woman customer may have in her life. For example, she may be trying to pick up her car as quickly as possible because she is running late in retrieving her kids from a day care that charges late fees by the minute.**

SAY

✓ **How can I help you get through the process faster, so that you can get on with what you need to do?**

DO

✓ **Offer to save the customer time by paying for her lunch or getting a cab for her, so she can run errands instead of waiting at the dealership.**

✓ **Work actively with the service department to ensure prompt attention to all of the customer's car problems.**

✓   Respond professionally and promptly to all of the customer's concerns in order to maintain a good relationship. Telephone calls should always be returned within three to four hours.

✓   Implement a tracking system to remember when to contact your customers.

✓   Consistently ensure that the customer is satisfied with each interaction with the dealership.

✓   *Treat her right.* Treat every customer as if she could be "the one," the customer who brings in more business than you ever believed possible!

✓   *Own your mistakes.* Customers appreciate it when sales professionals take responsibility for their actions. A simple but sincere apology goes much further than a dozen excuses or defensive reactions.

DON'T

✓   Mention private aspects of your life in order to win over her sympathies. It will simply make a woman customer uncomfortable, and it may cause you to lose the sale.

✓   "Plead poor." Don't say the special price you can offer is so low the dealership won't make any money on the deal. Then the customer will wonder, "Why make the deal at all?"

✓ **Force the issue. Don't try to back a woman into a corner to rush her decision. If you do, the decision will always be *no*.**

Chapter Seven

The Challenge

The following afternoon, both Holmes and I were at the car dealership again. He was not in costume this evening, nor was he going by Rollo Peppers, the ridiculous name he had manufactured for his previous stint as a salesperson. He had come back to the lot, hat literally in hand, and confessed his prior deception to the manager and his co-workers on the sales staff just as Lysette had requested.

Holmes told no lies to his former employer, but neither did he reveal every aspect of the case upon which we were working on. Discretion was the excuse given for certain omissions, which was true enough. But it wasn't only Wells that Holmes was now protecting; it was Lysette.

"Holmes, are you quite sure about this?" I asked, concerned for my friend. We had spent much of the

Illustration Number Five: Active Listening
*The key to creating any great plan for change is **active lis-***
***tening.** Holmes has gone to the expert, and he's hanging on*
Watson's every word of wisdom (all of which came from
women). A new plan is forming and success is on the horizon.

previous evening rehearsing this scenario, and all morning we prepared his dress and appearance. Holmes was determined to go through with Lysette's challenge. He seemed calm and focused, ready to prove he could right his past wrongs and prove to her that he could indeed change. Yet I still detected a touch of anxiety within him.

"Watson, did I ever tell you of the night I went to see the final exhibition bout of the great boxer Leonard Howe?"

I honestly couldn't recall. My eye drifted to a near-by clock. It was nearly time.

"I arrived early," Holmes continued, "and though I am loathe to use the celebrity status your accounts of our adventures has given me, I admit I did that night. As such, I was allowed to visit the boxers in their dressing rooms.

"Howe's competitor was my first stop. To tell you the truth, I was so unimpressed with him I cannot even recall his name. He was shaking hands, signing autographs, glorying in the attention. I lost interest in him immediately. Howe, on the other hand, was in the midst of serious training and could not stop rocking the bag, even to speak with a celebrated detective such as myself. The man's intensity and focus was a wonder to behold, an exciting spectacle that even his grand performances in the ring hardly matched."

"Yes," I said, recalling our own marathon preparations and the determined look I so often glimpsed in Holmes' eyes.

"His reputation was fixed," Holmes said fondly. "This match was simply to help place attention on a new ring a former opponent had built. The outcome hardly mattered. He was a champion and a champion he would remain, even if he was beaten in the first round. Yet that made no difference to him. He had the fire and determination of a hungry youth, the will of a timeless force of nature.

"In the years that followed the match, I kept close watch on him, and saw him apply that same energy and spirit to any and every enterprise he undertook. What more was there to give, when he had already given one-hundred percent?"

It was encouraging to know such moments were on Holmes' mind now. The seconds were ticking away. I heard footsteps on the pavement outside. Then came the distinctive click of a woman's heels.

Holmes heard it, too, and rose from the desk he had been assigned to cross the showroom and open the front door. A woman in a subdued black dress approached, a hat failing to cover much of her silky raven hair. Her features seemed plain, of makeup she wore very little. A few of the other salespeople watched her approach; most had their eyes on Holmes.

"There are two kinds of people in this world, Watson," Holmes said, "Some would climb halfway up a mountain, stop, and look down, thinking only about how far they have to fall. Others would look up happily, and see the wonders that lay ahead and the exciting challenges still before them. In the matter of adjusting to this new world of ours, of celebrating the differences rather than railing about them like an old fool, I have been the former. Today, I will learn if I can become the latter."

Holmes moved to greet the woman.

EDITORS' NOTES: IT'S ALL IN THE DETAILS

Now it's our turn to commend Holmes. We've been watching closely, and the parallel between making a sale and solving a mystery has become very clear to us. The first step in making a sale is to find out what the customer wants. It's the same as learning the details of the mystery that needs to be solved.

—R&M

"Good afternoon," Holmes said, holding the door for the woman. He smiled warmly. "My name is Sherlock Holmes. And you are?"

"Gretchen Ellis," she said hesitantly, though she took the hand he offered her. and seemed to appreciate his strong handshake. Her shoulders, which had been bunched defensively, eased a little. "Sherlock Holmes? Really? You wouldn't be having a bit of fun at my expense, would you?"

"Gretchen...may I call you Gretchen?" he asked.

"Yes."

"Holmes is the name I was born with. I can honestly say that it often thrusts me into interesting situations. But today, Gretchen, I am your humble servant. How can I help you?"

Won over by his charm and his genuine interest, Gretchen told Holmes that she was looking for a vehicle that she, as a widowed mother of two, not only could afford, but would help guarantee her family's safety on the busy streets of London. She was interested in practicality far more than appearance, and Holmes noted all of her concerns and desires, reflecting them back to her in conversation to verify that he understood her correctly, and to let her know that he had been paying attention to her every word.

He leaned in when she spoke, held her gaze while he was listening, and only talked when it was necessary.

EDITORS' NOTES: OPEN FOR BUSINESS

The second stage of a mystery is searching for clues. This is much the same as helping the customer find a good fit. Staying open to all the possibilities and really listening to the customer's feelings about each option is of critical importance.   —R&M

Holmes asked if Gretchen had been to other dealerships, and the woman frankly admitted that she had. Then he asked her why she had not purchased a vehicle from one of those other dealerships. The woman was extremely forthcoming, listing her dissatisfaction with the way she had been treated by certain salespeople, and the drawbacks of certain cars. By informing Holmes that a particular car from another dealership did not have enough leg room, she gave him a vital clue that leg room was a major consideration. This helped him narrow down the field of automobiles he might show her.

At another dealership, she felt unduly pressured when it came time to discuss the payment; this clued Holmes to apply as little pressure as possible when that time came in their transaction. By asking indirect questions, the detective gained more intelligence than if he had simply grilled the customer for information. And he was gaining valuable insight from the mistakes of others.

"Holmes, old boy, you're learning," I whispered.

Unlike Edward Merchance, I thought. Merchance was that salesperson whom Holmes had warned me about. As Merchance watched Holmes work, he told me that *he* would have handled Gretchen much differently.

"How?" I asked.

"I would have told her that I, too, was a single parent. And to further win over her sympathies, I would have talked about my son and mentioned some of the various trials I'd endured. Then I'd find out what her favorite meal was, and I'd schedule a little *detour* on our test drive for a spot of lunch and a chance to get to know her better."

I casually inquired as to how many women he had sold cars to using *this* method. His answer, of course, was *none*. But he had a ready excuse in each instance to explain why the fault did not lie at his doorstep.

I ignored the man from that point out and concentrated on Holmes, who was now leading the woman to the lot, and to one of several cars that he felt met her requirements.

I drifted outside to get a closer look, pleased to see Holmes giving Gretchen plenty of space, a primary consideration for women. Yet he remained close enough to be there and be of assistance when she expressed that want.

The woman spoke of price, and Holmes was up-front with her, eschewing many of the tactics he said he had heard Merchance using, including 'pleading poor' by saying the special price he could offer was so low, the dealership wouldn't be making any money on the deal. Instead, Holmes looked and acted like a true professional, his dress and manner clearly indicating that he respected his customer, her views, and her time.

She selected a vehicle for a test drive, and soon they were off. Inside, I heard one of the salesmen mutter that this would be the end of the matter, that Holmes couldn't sell a glass of water to a dying man in the desert. Several days ago, I might have agreed. Now, I was filled with optimism, which I kept to myself as part of the plan to which we had agreed upon.

Of course, I could not accompany the two of them on the test drive, so I have no idea what Holmes and the woman discussed. Nor was he forthcoming with details later. I can only say that when they returned, both seemed relaxed and certain that this was the car that would best meet her needs.

Needless to say, the salespeople on the floor were astounded. I withheld my own accolades, because this process was far from over.

EDITORS' NOTES: PUTTING IT ALL TOGETHER

The third stage of solving a mystery is putting all the clues together to find the solution. In car sales terms, taking the customer inside, keeping them enthusiastic, and making the numbers work.   —R&M

Holmes reentered the dealership and immediately announced that he was with a very important customer and was not to be disturbed under any circumstances. This was a wise move for many reasons. It let the woman know that she was his one and only concern, and it eliminated the possibility that he would be interrupted by a phone call or other inquiry.

Holmes led the woman to an office that had been temporarily assigned to him. He sat with her for nearly half-an-hour, explaining every option available to her in the purchasing process. He even went so far as to consult with the finance manager to create a *final* figure for her—including the warranty and other options she might wish to pursue, and the exact worth of her trade-in.

EDITORS' NOTES: SEAL THE DEAL

Finally, one must solve the mystery, or close the deal. In mysteries, this usually means a dramatic confrontation. In a sales scenario, particularly with women, the least amount of drama, the better.   —R&M

Holmes broached the potentially touchy subject of whether or not all the principles were present by asking, "Are there any other things to consider before we start getting the car ready for you?" Then he asked, "Is there any other information you need to make *your* decision?" Holmes followed that question up with, "Are we ready to sign the papers?"

The intent was clear. By asking questions phrased in this manner, he was giving her every opportunity to volunteer the information he required, rather than making her feel pressured by questions that suggested that she was not empowered.

This was a highly effective example of *pressure-less closing.* Holmes understood that the worst possible move he could make would have been to back the woman into a corner. He knew from experience that she would turn and run and not come back. The woman had no desire to have her precious time wasted. By the same

Illustration Number Six: Executing

Success! Holmes has not only sold a car, he has made a cus-
*tomer for life. He is still in the **executing** stage of change,*
wherein he will always be honing his skills and practicing
the craft of selling to women. And he won't succeed every
time. But with constant striving comes consistent improve-
ment. Good show, Holmes!

token, she did not want to be rushed into a decision. The first time she asked for time to think things over, Holmes backed off and offered her that time—well aware that she was much more likely to come back to him if she did not feel pressured.

Holmes then suggested that since it would take time to get the paperwork together and the automobile ready for her inspection, if she were so inclined, she may journey to a restaurant across the street and have lunch on him. He wrote her a note to give to the manager, charging her meal to his account. Pleasantly surprised, the woman took him up on his generous offer.

When Gretchen returned, she spoke to Holmes within earshot of the other salespeople. "I want you to understand something. I'm buying from you because you took the time to listen to what I had to say, to tell me what I needed to know, and you had the consideration to ask me what I thought, to understand and respect my opinion."

Holmes glanced my way, and I could not help but beam with pride and pleasure over what he had accomplished. Our new world would no longer be an alien place to him, and progress would certainly mean opportunity and adventure.

EDITORS' NOTES: LET THEM TELL YOU

A third or more of women customers who buy a car from you will volunteer their reason why they are buying from you, letting you know what you did right. This kind of direct feedback is rarely given by men. Women often make their buying decisions based on the quality of the relationship that is initiated with the salesperson; whereas, men typically do not.   —R&M

Holmes offered Gretchen a small stack of business cards, asking her to distribute them to friends who might be interested in purchasing automobiles. The woman took them gladly, stating that it would be her pleasure. Referrals are a major source of new clientele in the world of detection, and the automotive business was no different.

EDITORS' NOTES: NETWORKING

The idea that women network constantly can work for or against a salesperson. Women are just as likely to discuss a bad experience and warn off their friends as they are to talk about a good experience and pass along a business card.   —R&M

The woman departed in her new vehicle. The sales-people—with the exception of Merchance—were so impressed with Holmes' performance that they interro-gated him about his technique for several hours, taking detailed notes and asking many questions. But before this process was undertaken, Holmes engaged the serv-ices of a messenger to leave a note at the woman's door, thanking her for her business and entreating her to call upon him whenever he could be of assistance.

I slipped away, walking for several blocks to a pre-determined spot where the woman waited with her new vehicle.

"Have you derived satisfaction?" I asked.

Lysette took off her hat and wig and stated that she had.

"Meet me at Mr. Wells' home tonight, and I shall help you in whatever manner I can."

Chapter Seven Checklist

COMPETENCIES EXPLORED IN THIS CHAPTER

✓ **Establish a Trusting Relationship.**
✓ **Uncover Her Specific Needs and Wants.**
✓ **Make a Professional Sales Presentation.**
✓ **Complete a Pressure-less Closing.**
✓ **Build an Enhanced Relationship with Her and Hers.**
✓ **Provide Efficient, Non-Intrusive Administration.**

COMPETENCIES—*collections of observable behaviors in categories that, when demonstrated, indicate a level of successful performance.*

BEHAVIORS—*each competency is followed by a series of phrases that describe actions (or behaviors) characteristic of a person who performs with a high degree of ability in that area. The behaviors will be demonstrated, in varying degrees, by those with different abilities and positions.*

KEEP IN MIND

✓ **There is a parallel between making a sale and solving a mystery.**

✓ **The first step is to find out what the customer wants. It's the same as learning the details of the mystery that needs to be solved.**

✓   The second stage of a mystery is searching for clues. This is much the same as helping the customer find a good fit. Be open to all the possibilities, and really listen to the customer's feelings about each option. This is of critical importance.

✓   The third stage of solving a mystery is putting all the clues together to find the solution. In car sales terms, take the customer inside, keep them enthusiastic, and make the numbers work.

✓   Finally, one must solve the mystery, or close the deal. In mysteries, this usually means a dramatic confrontation. In a sales scenario, particularly with women, the least amount of drama, the better.

THINK

✓   *Let them give me the answers.* Two-thirds or more of women customers who buy a car from me will volunteer the reasons why they are (or are not) buying from me, letting me know up front what I did right or wrong. This is a great opportunity for me because this kind of direct feedback is rarely given by men. I must remember that women often make their buying decisions based on the quality of the relationship that is initiated with the salesperson; whereas, men typically do not.

✓ *Networking.* The women's network can work for me. Women are just as likely to discuss a bad experience with me and warn off friends as they are to talk about a good experience with me and pass along my business card.

DO

✓ Ask if she has been to other dealerships. Use what she tells you to your advantage.

✓ Ask direct questions.

Act like a champion. Love what you do and go the extra mile every time. That includes:

✓ Greeting her politely.

✓ Giving her a firm handshake.

✓ Showing a genuine interest in what she wants and needs out of a car.

✓ Giving her plenty of space when walking—around the car lot, but remaining close enough so that you can be there and be of assistance when she has a question.

✓ Noting all of her concerns and desires. Reflect them back to her in conversation to verify that you understand her correctly. This will also let her know that you have been paying attention to her every word.

✓ Leaning in when she speaks to show that you are listening.

✓ Maintaining eye contact.

✓ Talking only when necessary.

✓ Learning from the mistakes of others.

✓ Being up-front about the price of the car.

✓ Dressing and acting like a true professional. Show in your manner and the way you speak that you respect your customer, her views, and her time.

✓ Taking the time to go over options. Make sure she isn't going to get any surprises that might upset the deal you've worked so hard to create. Sit down with her and explain every option available to her in the purchasing process.

✓ *Letting her work with one person.* Consult with the finance manager to create a final figure for the customer, including the warranty and other options she might wish to pursue and the exact worth of her trade-in. The last thing a woman wants is to be handed off to another, unfamiliar person at the critical point in a transaction.

✓ Letting her think about her decision. If she asks for time to think things through give her the time and space required.

✓ Taking her to lunch, but stay behind. Once the sale is made, all that's left for the customer is lost time waiting around while the paper-

work and the car are prepared. Set up a tab at a nearby restaurant and let her go to lunch on you.

✓ Going the extra mile—over the phone. Leave a phone message on the woman customer's answering machine right after she leaves the dealership. Thank her for her business and ask her to call whenever you can be of assistance. She's bound to be impressed and appreciate the gesture.

✓ Building an after sale ongoing meaningful follow-up system that is non-intrusive yet responsive that promotes a long term professional relationship.

Chapter Eight

The Mystery is Solved

L ysette met us at Wells' home promptly at eight that evening. The eager writer led her to the cluttered office where he and Dooley spent so much time. She said hardly a word, surveying instead the mess with an eye that appeared as trained and discerning as Holmes'.

At last, she approached the wall of reference texts, studying the bindings of one after another, until she pulled one down and opened it—revealing the very prize Wells had sought.

"I don't understand!" Wells exclaimed. "The manuscript was *here* all along!"

Lysette nodded. "Jonathan said that you were concerned over having your work stolen. I know him well enough to understand how he thinks, and by putting myself in his shoes, I decided he must have hidden the manuscript for safekeeping—which he did by removing the pages from the binding of this book and replacing them with your manuscript pages.

I also know that he tries to avoid confrontations at all costs, which explains his abrupt departure. Further, I know him to be absent-minded, which is undoubtedly why he forgot to tell you where he had placed the manuscript so that thieves might not notice it."

"Then where is Mr. Dooley?" I asked.

"On a boat to the states, I would venture," Holmes said.

Lysette turned, surprised, but only for a moment.

"You learned that he has relatives there, didn't you, Mr. Holmes?" Lysette guessed. "Wealthy ones that he sought to petition for loftier connections, leaving me behind."

"Sorrowfully, yes," Holmes said, and the regret tingeing his voice was sincere.

"Life here is a struggle, I admit," said Lysette with a sigh, "but I told him on many occasions that I would marry him and together we could stay true to our dreams, strive to achieve excellence through our own hard work, build a life to be proud of rather than beg for crumbs from rich relatives. He did not listen. Did not believe. So I let him go. It was all I could do."

Illustration Number Seven: Embedding
Holmes has reached the final stage of change. His new behaviors have firmly taken hold and he can't believe he ever treated women customers any other way. Even Mrs. Hudson is happy! The **embedding** stage of change also requires practice and long-term attendance, but the results are dramatic and consistent. Holmes has solved the mystery!

And with that, we allowed Lysette to leave. Just before exiting the small office, she turned to Holmes and promised that she would keep in touch, entreating him to do the same.

He said that he would, and both kept their promises, developing a friendship that was profitable indeed as she referred many clients his way. Her friendship and insight paved the way to knowledge and an even brighter future than expected for a man whose brilliance would, I firmly believe, touch every age.

EDITORS' NOTES: MORE TOOLS

In sales and service (and always remember that service is sales) the goal should always be to forge lifelong relationships with customers.

—R&M

You've lived the mystery, and along the way you've benefited from the many valuable Editors' Notes throughout Watson's narrative. You've watched Sherlock Holmes progress from the master detective without a clue (at least where women are concerned) to a genuinely caring, empathetic, and respectful salesperson who knows how to sell cars to women.

You may think you've learned everything you need to know, but you're not out of the woods yet. What you've learned so far will have you primed to be incredibly successful selling to women. But there are more insights to be gained, more techniques to be learned. Holmes discovered how to become a *very good* salesperson.

You're about to learn how to become a *champion*.

PART THREE

Resources for Champion Salespeople

Voice of the Customer

Wouldn't you like to know what women are saying behind your back? Well, get ready. You are about to hear just that.

The following observations and comments were taken from two focus groups, each comprised of 10 women who had two things in common: First, each had purchased either a new or used car, domestic or foreign, in the last six months. Second, none of them particularly enjoyed the process.

You are about to learn precisely what women like and dislike about the car buying experience. The comments by the women and their detailed description of their experiences will provide your sales and service people with insights into how they can increase their

closing ratios and nail perfect "5" C.S.I.s every time with your women customers.

One final point (that is sure to scream out to you as much as it did to us): When a woman enters your store, she is shopping for a car for herself and her family. She has done the research, she knows what she does and does not want, and her significant other is rarely involved in the final decision. As a result of culling the data from these focus groups, we discovered that few sales and service people in the automotive industry understand this point. After reading these comments, you will.

RESPECT? WHAT'S THAT?

SHE'S JUST A ONE-LEGGER

"I walked into a dealership, a woman on my own, and no one would take me seriously. I'm pulling down more money, every year, than any of these salespeople, but I was told to bring my husband in when I was serious."

—Theresa, 31, single

THE WALLET'S WHAT MATTERS, NOT THE POCKETBOOK

"Salesmen need to understand that even if my husband is filling out the paperwork and purchasing the car, he, most likely, is not the one who's going to drive it, he is *not* the one with the final say. If I don't like the car, if I'm not satisfied, the sale isn't happening. Period."

—Carolyn, 38, mother of two

WHAT WOMEN *HATE* ABOUT BUYING A CAR

SEE CUSTOMER, LEAP ON CUSTOMER

"I drove onto the lot with my husband and the salesman immediately jumped on us. We didn't even have a chance to take a breath, let alone look around. As soon as we got out of the car, here he comes out the door. I rolled my eyes and said to my husband, 'Oh, boy, here we go...'"

—Sandra, 28, married with one child

BUY NOW! BUY NOW!

"When we walked in, there was enormous pressure to buy right then and there. 'Don't leave. Don't go anyplace else. Don't look at anything else. We want you to buy this car right now.' That made me nervous and uncomfortable, so I turned around and walked out."

—Jane, 32, married

OUR BEST DEAL

"They treat you like you're stupid. Right from the beginning, it's one big game. 'This price is the best we can do.' 'Let me tell you, we aren't making *any* money on this.' 'This is our absolute, positive, best deal ever...' Yeah, right, until you say, 'no,' then there's another price, and another one, and another one. It's ridiculous. They just show you they're lying. Why would anyone with an ounce of brains put up with that?"

—Marie, 43, married with three children

LOOK HER IN THE EYE? WHAT'S UP WITH THAT?

"One salesman we had was not comfortable talking to women and would only make eye contact with my husband. I was buying this car. It was *my* choice. But this salesman wouldn't answer my questions, wouldn't look me in the eye, and this was after myself and my husband both told him, 'You're making a mistake, you're talking to the wrong person.' And he kept right on doing it. That was the end of it. I walked out the door, my husband right behind me…. I'd had it!"

—Lysette, 30, married with two children

HURRY UP AND WAIT

"After we decided to purchase the car, we were probably there for another four hours, and that was ridiculous."

—Cassandra, 25, married

THE CAUTIOUS BUYER

"I only brought my husband because I thought *maybe* they wouldn't try to cheat me if he was there. Maybe."

—Carrie, 49, married with three children

RESEARCH TELLS

"I researched what my car was worth on the Internet and with the current Blue Book, as we were going to trade it in. When they tried to give us like $500.00 for my car, I put the paperwork I'd gathered up on his desk and said, 'I don't think so.'"

—Linda, 28, married

WHAT WOMEN *LOVE* ABOUT BUYING A CAR

R-E-S-P-E-C-T

"The last time I bought a car and was happy with the salesperson was when I went in and told this guy, 'You have *one hour* to give us the best price.' He did. No runaround. No treating me like I was an idiot. No playing games. I'll go back to him any day."

—Traci, 23, single

NO GAMES, JUST SPORTS

"I said, 'Here is what we can afford. Go to your manager and give me your best price because I have my daughter at home with my mom, I have to put her to bed in an hour, and I can't stay. Then the manager came out and shook my hand and said, 'What can you afford?' I said, 'No, you tell me what the best price is.' He came back and said, 'This is the best that we can do.' We had a number in mind, and he was within $10.00 of that. We drove the car home an hour later."

—Melissa, 35, married with one child

BY THE BOOK

"I took my computer print out with me to the dealer. I just pulled it right out and said "I got this off the

Internet" and told him what we wanted to pay for the car and he went along with it. It was the smoothest sale I have ever made. Simple, clear, and away we go! He even went the extra mile to get the color and everything that I wanted. They had to get a car from out of state, and they drove it in and called me when it arrived. I would go to him again in a heartbeat."

—Kelly, 36, single

GOOD NEWS OR BAD, WOMEN TELL ALL

TELL ALL YOUR FRIENDS

"I told everyone I knew that I had a good car buying experience. I mean, I had an absolutely perfect experience. The salesman gave me a stack of cards, and I told him that I appreciated him being honest about everything. I passed out his cards to all my friends, to everyone I work with, to anyone I thought might be looking to buy a car."

—Justine, 27, married

BAD NEWS TRAVELS FAST

"Our car-buying experience was so bad that I made sure everyone at work, everyone at the stylists, everyone at my daughter's school, everyone at church, everyone I could get to listen, knew exactly which dealership they should stay away from and why."

—Ellen, 31, married with one child

DEALERSHIP AVOIDANCE

GOOD SUNDAY

"We like to go to car lots on a Sunday when no one is there. Then you don't have to deal with salesmen. They are usually right on top of you before you can even take a breath. Then, when you want somebody to help you, you can't find anyone. If I have to do it myself, I'd just as soon do it on my terms, without being harassed."

—Martine, 45, married with two children

HOW WOMEN DO AND DON'T WANT TO BE TREATED

HEY, BABY

"I had a salesman hit on me. I decided to go elsewhere. He asked me for a dinner date, and I didn't to go to dinner. I wanted to buy a car. I just wanted to go in, get a car, and leave. He called me 'baby,' 'honey,' and 'sweetie,' all in the span of about five minutes. Then he told me that if things got tight, he would take me out to dinner."

—Laura, 24, married

ON THE CLOCK

"I want to be treated like my time is just as valuable as the salesperson's time. Because it is."

—Rachel, 29, single

THE PRODUCT SELLS ITSELF, DON'T GET IN THE WAY

"I like it when the car salespeople are laid back and they come up to you and say, "That's a really good choice, do you want to take it for a drive?' I'm a lot more likely to buy when I feel like they're not trying to sell me anything. The car, its quality, and its price...that's what's going to sell me. That and being treated well."

—Courtney, 34, married with one child

SALES IS SERVICE

IT IS YOUR PROBLEM

"My vehicle was six months old when it just died. The service department told me they were going to have to replace the engine, and I freaked out and said 'You have got to be kidding me. What am I going to do?' and he said, 'That's not our problem.' I got the State Attorney's office involved and *made* it their problem. Then I never went back there again."

—Michelle, 39, married

SERVICE MAKES OR BREAKS A SALE

"If you are teetering on the edge of going with a particular dealership or not, and you know their service stinks, you're going to sign with the competition. But if they show they really care about you and you are comfortable with their reassurances, you are more likely to stay on board with them."

—Susan, 25, single

MORE IS MORE

"I'd rather pay more for a car and get good service than take a better deal and get lousy service."

—Georgette, 35, married with two children

OTHER IMPORTANT MESSAGES

WOMEN BUY CARS FOR DIFFERENT REA-
SONS THAN MEN.

One woman bought an SUV for carpooling, so she
and other mothers could take their children to events
and activities together.

One woman bought a car with a lot of room because
she has three sons who constantly fight and they need
to be separated.

Most women drive because they have somewhere
they need to be, a task that must be performed (however, more and more women are buying cars for leisure or
as symbols of status).

WOMEN BUY CARS IN DIFFERENT WAYS
THAN MEN.

One woman knew exactly what kind of car she
wanted and called all the local dealerships asking if
they had that car in stock. Only *one* called her back to
let her know that they would have it soon, and then they
called her when it came in.

Women prefer a low-pressure sale to a high-pres-
sure one. They move away from "pressure."

Women use the Internet and their own personal network of friends and associates to do their research

ahead of time in an attempt to make the buying process quick and painless. Women hate to get the runaround or to be talked down to.

Most women have had negative experiences buying cars, so be aware that many may walk into your store with a chip on their shoulders—and understandably so. But you can be the one to knock that chip off, and create a customer for life—*if* you listen.

So now you've heard the actual words of women car-buyers. You have a better idea of your goal during the sales process: Conduct yourself in ways that will make women want to forge a lifetime buying relationship with you.

But *how* do you do that?

We've talked to many of the top performers in the car business, and we've discovered that they all follow the same set of rules. Experience has taught them the right way to act with women car-buyers in order to A) make the sale every time, B) become the one and only person that the woman customer considers contacting for other vehicle purchases, and C) have women car-buyers recommend them to their friends.

You'd think they all shared the same playbook!

Well...now they do. We've gathered all of their very best strategies for selling cars to women and boiled them down to the pages you're about to read. We've put these strategies (core competencies) into the same format that the top brass of major corporations pay consultants big bucks to write—so don't let the language throw you.

Here are the terms that you will need to know:

Competency Model—a collection of the behaviors, characteristics, and attributes that differentiate the top performers in your field.

Competencies—collections of observable behaviors in categories that, when demonstrated, indicate a level of successful performance.

Behaviors—each competency is followed by a series of phrases that describe actions (or behaviors) characteristic of a person who performs with a high degree of ability in that area. The behaviors will be demonstrated, in varying degrees, by those with different abilities and positions.

There are examples of things to do with women customers listed with each competency that are printed in bold and bracketed by dark lines.

You're about to look at the kind of thing your bosses might use to evaluate your performance on the job. As an added bonus, we've supplied some notes to make these strategies even more understandable.

Think of the following section—"The Six Competencies of Top Producers"—as your personal "cheat sheet" for getting RICH selling cars to women!

The Six Competencies for Top Producers

1. ESTABLISH A TRUSTING RELATIONSHIP

The champion salesperson—

Works actively with the customer to deliver a shopping and buying experience in which the customer wants to participate.

Ask the customer how you can help her today. Ask her name and the name of her companion if she is accompanied.

Demonstrates flexibility by listening to and respecting the customer's desired outcome (e.g., the woman customer may only be gathering data for comparison or to share with her spouse, but she must be treated well; otherwise, she may not return to purchase. The rule 'off-the-lot means never-to-return' does not generally apply to women. Perhaps she has only a limited amount of time she is willing or able to spend on this process.)

Responds professionally and promptly to customer concerns; resolves problems and maintains an effective working relationship.

Consistently transcends the product category to become a "trusted" advisor.

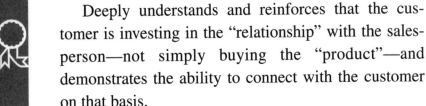

Invite her to walk around by herself and contact you when she has a question, needs help, or before she has to leave.

Deeply understands and reinforces that the customer is investing in the "relationship" with the salesperson—not simply buying the "product"—and demonstrates the ability to connect with the customer on that basis.

Listens well to customer concerns, immediately clarifies misunderstandings, and follows up on all customer concerns until customer expectations are surpassed.

Take notes of important information and maintain eye contact with the customer to show active listening.

References other success stories, common experiences, people and organizations in the community.

2. UNCOVER HER SPECIFIC NEEDS AND WANTS

The champion salesperson—

Uses the customer's past history with cars to pinpoint her specific needs and identify her specific issues to prepare a thorough sales presentation and make the sale.

Asks well-crafted questions about the customer's needs without invading her personal space or creating a sense of urgency.

Discover what ways the customer will use the car and whether she has a specific budget allocated.

Demonstrates the ability to listen without preparing to talk.

Records information, impressions, and personal data volunteered by the customer that can be used to build a long-term relationship after the sale.

Evaluate what is most important to her about the car: Safety? Reliability? Gas Mileage? Warrantee? Etc.

Reflects understanding of needs and wants back to the customer after taking in both what is said and what is unsaid and makes sure the customer agrees with the assessment.

3. MAKE A PROFESSIONAL SALES PRESENTATION

The champion salesperson—

Delivers the sales presentation in a configuration most important to the customer, demonstrating flexibility in modifying the presentation based on the customer's requirements.

Utilizes appropriate selling tools and marketing materials to differentiate themselves, their company, and their product from the competition.

Reference the convenience and reliability of your service department and your willingness to stick with the customer from sale to service.

Matches the prospective customer with the best fit of product, price, and promotion available.

Shows concern about the totality of the customer's product ownership cycle, from sale to service to trade-in and upgrade.

Personally review all financial options with the customer.

Exudes professionalism in personal appearance, demeanor, environment, conversations, and actions.

Dedicates self to continually upgrading all sales and service skills, particularly people skills.

4. COMPLETE A PRESSURE-LESS CLOSING

The champion salesperson—

Puts the customer's needs first and allows her to close now, or take the time to think about the purchase decision.

Demonstrates the ability to follow up without making the customer feel pressured.

Move the sales process along as speedily as possible (once the customer has decided to purchase) so that you do not waste the customer's time.

Understands that the customer may not complete the purchase on the first visit, and develops an action plan for follow-up with the customer. (And understands that she may need to gather information, read information, digest the information, ask more questions, collaborate with friends and family before completing the sale.)

Works actively with the customer to assist her in the decision-making process by offering to provide additional information or materials.

Act as intermediary with the finance department to ensure that the customer understands and agrees to the total cost of the deal.

Facilitates the customer making "right" decisions for her around all purchase criteria, including timing, budgets, product, annual costs, etc.

Shows no sense of anxiety around the customer's decision-making process to purchase or not to purchase immediately.

Declares to the customer the desire and willingness to earn her business, and is comfortable putting her pressing needs above an immediate sale to foster a long-term relationship.

5. BUILD AN ENHANCED RELATIONSHIP WITH HER AND HERS

The champion salesperson—

Identifies self as the control center for providing customer satisfaction. Brings other people into the mix as required to exceed customer expectations through the product's useful life.

Actively monitors customer activity on a regular basis, and works with service as required to seize opportunities and/or deal directly with problems that may arise.

Facilitate interactions with the service department.

Focuses on earning and acquiring repeat business, and understands that repeat business is secured based on what happens *after* the sale.

Understands word-of-mouth referrals are the foundation to building a large customer base. Works hard to leverage every contact into multiple referrals.

Develops ways to connect regularly with buyers, prospects, and their networks.

Offer to send the customer a monthly newsletter with interesting facts for women as a way of discreetly keeping the lines of communication open with the customer after the sale is completed.

Updates and maintains customer information frequently.

Follows up on customer's commitment with a visit or telephone call one week after sale to ensure that the customer is delighted with the purchase—or to help the customer solve problems.

Recognizes and values every opportunity to talk to the customer or prospect in an effort to build relationships, gathering additional information about needs and wants, becoming the one and only choice for referrals.

Works hard to demonstrate to the customer that she is never alone in the process. Keeps all promises made during the sales phase.

6. PROVIDE EFFICIENT, NON-INTRUSIVE ADMINISTRATION

The champion salesperson—

Consistently ensures that the customer is satisfied with each and every interaction with the dealership.

When beginning the administration process—contracts and paperwork associated with the process of the customer buying the car—offer to save the customer time by buying her lunch with her children, sending her by cab to get an errand done, et cetera.

Works actively with the service department to ensure prompt attention to the customer's service problems.

Returns all calls to the customer within three hours and always on the same day the call was received.

Creates a monitoring system to increase efficiency in responding to customer requests and maintaining contacts.

Consistently ensures that the customer is satisfied with each interaction with the dealership.

Never wastes the customer's time and makes elapsed time invisible to the customer.

Now you've seen the plays used by the champion salespeople, the best of the best. But there's a big difference between reading strategies in a book and putting them into play in your everyday life. *You* have to change the way you're doing things, and that can be hard. But it can also pay off for you if you learn to move more cars every month and get RICH selling cars to women!

This next section—"Now That I Know What To Do... How Do I Do It"—will give you a step by step guide to making the fundamental changes in your life that will help you achieve this goal-or any other.

You can do it!

Now That I Know What To Do... How Do I Do It?

Great news! You are *already* on step three of a five step process that will help you get RICH selling cars to women. The women's market is huge, and yet there are still many salespeople who pretend that it doesn't exist. But you know better, and that puts you ahead of the curve. Don't stop now! You are poised to uncover the last few pieces of the puzzle. You are ready to create a plan and put it into action.

Choose Your Improvement

Now that you have read the Six Competencies of Top Producers, you're ready to start putting these plays from the expert playbook into action so you can improve your sales with women customers. We admire your determination to be the best car salesperson you can be. We also know that we've given you a lot of information. The question is, where do you start?

Chances are you are *already* expertly employing some of these six critical strategies of selling cars to women; and, for that reason, you won't need to work on all six competencies and their accompanying behaviors.

For example, you may be highly skilled at greeting women when they come into the dealership but find pressure-less closing very difficult. This section is designed to help you identify those two or three competencies (and the few behaviors under each competency you have chosen) where you may need improvement, so you can sell that one additional car a month—and start down that road to riches!

Think about your improvement in these terms: What if you did just three things differently? For example, let's say you wanted to improve your golf game. Here are three things you might do:

1. Change your grip. This would dramatically improve your game.

2. Learn how to come out of the sand. This would save you a double stroke.

3. Become a strong a putter. This would improve your score.

If you changed these three things in your golf game, then perhaps you would finally break 100.

IMPROVEMENT EXERCISE

1. Review the Six Competencies of Top Producers and choose one on which you feel you need to work.

2. Choose three behaviors under that competency in which you would like to perform with greater skill.

3. Write your three choices down in this book so you can keep track of the behaviors on which you are working.

BEHAVIORS TO CHANGE

1. _____

2. _____

3. _____

Getting Started

Now that you have made a list of the three behaviors that you want to change, it's time to create a game plan for accomplishing that goal. Think of these old behaviors as habits. To break yourself of these old habits, substitute new ones. In order to do this, be very specific about what the new habit is going to be. For example, if you usually greet a woman who comes onto your lot by saying: "What car can I show you today?" and you decide to use a different phrase, then you need to work out the wording for that new phrase ahead of time. Let's say that the new phrase you decide to use will be: "How can I be most helpful to you today?"

Once you've made this decision, it's time to warm up by getting together any possible related intelligence that will help you change your behavior. For example, ask your wife, your daughter, and any woman family members to tell you about positive sales experiences that they have had so you can use that information to help you achieve your goal. Their insights may assist you in deciding *how* you are going to deliver your new phrase.

Naturally, before going into the dealership and trying your new behavior (your new habit/new opening line) on a woman customer, there is one more thing to do—practice.

You can practice with your wife, your daughter, and woman friends/family members: the same people who helped you with their insights previously. You might also want to practice in front of a mirror to make sure that you look comfortable and relaxed when speaking this phrase, which is new to you.

Once you are comfortable using the phrase with family and friends, you can then begin using it in the work setting.

PLANNING EXERCISE

1. Decide who can help you practice your new behaviors outside of the workplace. With whom can you practice and not be embarrassed? Who can you trust to give you an honest opinion about how you are doing?

2. Decide who can help you in the dealership by observing your new behavior on the job and giving you feedback. This person can be your sales manager, a fellow salesperson, or anyone who works at the dealership who can watch your interactions with women customers.

3. Take the three behaviors you wrote down in the first improvement exercise and copy them to the FROM section in this exercise.

4. For each of the three behaviors write down an alternate behavior in the three TO sections in the exercise. For example:

FROM: What car can I show you today?

TO: How can I be most helpful to you today?

FROM: Where is your husband so he can decide if you can buy this car?

TO: Do you want to buy this car?

NEW BEHAVIORS

FROM: _____

TO: _____

FROM: _____

TO: _____

FROM: _____

TO: _____

Being Realistic

You have now decided what three behaviors you want to change and planned new behaviors with which to replace them. The time has come to execute your changed behaviors. Here are some things to keep in mind as you are putting your new behaviors into action:

There will be a period of trial and error when you are implementing your changed behaviors. The important thing to remember is that, like learning a new golf swing, it takes time for you and your body to get the rhythm of the new behavior/swing. You will not be perfect the first time you use your new behaviors with a woman customer.

There will be times when you will do everything properly, but your efforts still won't succeed with a woman customer. Don't take this as a failure. Remember that some women prefer buying from women salespeople; and, no matter what a male salesperson does, he will not get the sale. It is not a reflection on you.

There will be times when you relapse and accidentally use your old behaviors with women customers because you are so comfortable with them. For example, a friend of ours took a "Natural Golf" lesson to improve her game. After the lesson, our friend was convinced that this lesson was really going to help her game. Unfortunately, she wasn't able to get onto the golf course for a month. When she finally did, her golf game was the same as before because she had relapsed into all of her old swings. So don't give up. Relapse is a normal part of changing any behavior. The process of change will get easier.

After you have been trying your new behaviors for about a week, look at what worked with women customers—and what didn't—so you can revise your plan accordingly. For example, if there was a certain new phrase that you were using that didn't go over well with women, consider changing it to something else.

EXECUTING EXERCISE

1. Review the results for the past week's contacts with women customers.

2. Write down what new behaviors worked with women customers in the WHAT WORKED section of the exercise.

3. Write down what behaviors didn't work with women customers in the WHAT DIDN'T WORK section of the exercise.

4. For each of the behaviors that didn't work, write down an alternate behavior in the ALTERNATE BEHAVIOR section of the exercise.

CUSTOMER RESULTS

WHAT WORKED: ————————————————

————————————————————————

WHAT DIDN'T WORK: _____

_____

ALTERNATE BEHAVIOR: _____

_____

Practice Makes Perfect

Well done! You may have had a few false starts and a couple of relapses, but now you are using your new behaviors all the time. However, that is not the end of your road to long term change. These new behaviors are not yet permanently embedded into your routine.

You have to keep working at it. Keeping new behaviors is like retaining muscle tone. If you don't use your new behaviors/muscles often, you lose them. If you practice them on a regular basis, they become natural and automatic. This is what is known as muscle memory with professional athletes (your muscles remember what to do so you no longer have to think about what you are doing). The same idea applies to new behaviors.

Think of Michael Jordan and his famous jump shot. He has practiced that shot to the point that the movements have become a part of him. But he still goes on the court and practices before each and every game.

There are still other things you can do to improve your selling abilities with women customers. They include:

1. Constantly updating your skills. (There are always new things to learn, and you should take advantage of every opportunity to expand your knowledge base.)

2. Continue to up the ante of your sales to women customers. (If during the first month you use our lessons you sell one car to a woman customer, strive to sell two the next month and so on. Don't be satisfied with just one sale per month.)

3. Strive for greater CSI scores. (There is always more you can do for a customer to make them happy. Go beyond the ordinary to be the truly exceptional car salesperson.)

KEEPING TRACK OF YOUR SUCCESS EXERCISE

1. How many women customers did you work with this week? Write down that number in the WOMEN CUSTOMERS section of the exercise

2. Imagine that you worked with ten women customers this week. Think about how you dealt with these women customers. How often did you use your new behaviors with women customers?

3. What new behaviors did you try with these women? Write these new behaviors down in the NEW BEHAVIORS section of the exercise.

4. Under the KEEP TRACK section of the exercise, put a check mark in a box for each woman with whom you used new behaviors. For example, if you used new behaviors with three of your women customers, then it would look like this:

☑☑☑☐☐☐☐☐☐☐

5. Look at how many sales you had this week. How many male customers did you close? How many women customers did you close? Write down how many male customers you closed for a week in the MEN SOLD section of the exercise. Write down how many women customers you closed for a week in the WOMEN SOLD section of the exercise. After six weeks look at how many more women customers you are closing than male customers.

EMBEDDING EXERCISE

WOMEN CUSTOMERS ———

NEW BEHAVIORS ————————————

————————————————

KEEP TRACK   □□□□□□□□□□

MEN SOLD _____

WOMEN SOLD _____

NOTE: Photocopy these exercises and use them to follow your progress as your skills increase with women customers. You will be able to watch as all of your numbers go up, including the number of women customers you see every week and especially the number of women customers that you close.

And keep in mind, the exercises in this chapter make up only a small part of the overall MaddoxSmye training system.

To help you see what progress you've already made, we've created a chart describing the five step process of change. The simple fact that you've bought this book means you're already at stage three (where we began this chapter). That means you already recognize that you want to make a specific positive change in the way you approach selling cars to women and were looking for a plan. With this book, you've got one. Use this chart to remind yourself how far you've come.

Stages of Change

1. Ignoring—You do not recognize there is a problem.

2. Attending—You see the need for change, but continue with your current behavior.

3. Planning—You decide to change and plan how you're going to do it.

4. Executing—Your day-to-day activities start to change. Trial and error. Many successes.

5. Embedding—You wonder how you ever did it any other way.

Remember, practice makes perfect. Reaping the rewards from change requires planning and perseverance—traits you will profit from as you become a champion salesperson.

The Final Word

Now that we've come to the finish line with this book, we can't help but think about all the other great stories, teachings, statistics, trends, tips, and more that we would still like to share with you. That's why we'd like to make you an offer. Share with us your success with selling to women. Send us one story, one experience you have had, one question, one tip that has made an impact on you, along with your e-mail address, and we will send you sample copies of our newsletters *How to Sell to Women* and *Fast Facts and Tidbits*. These newsletters contain actionable tips you can use every day when selling to women.

In this way, we can continue learning from all of you on the front line while we share with you all of our "stuff" that didn't get into the book. Sounds like a winning strategy!

Contact us in any way that fits your style:

By mail: 300 Fifth Ave South, Suite 101, Box 420,
            Naples, Florida34102
By telephone: (416) 483-3955 or (203) 733-0665
By fax: (239)774-4858 or (416) 483-5085
By email: rmaddox@maddoxsmye.com
            msmye@maddoxsmye.com

We hope you've enjoyed and profited from Watson's account. Or, as Holmes would say, "The mystery is solved!"

Rebecca Maddox & Marti Smye

Acknowledgments

In one of our speeches we remarked, "No one achieves personal greatness alone. We achieve our personal greatness with and through others." We need to express our heartfelt thanks to all of those around us who have contributed to this book.

We thank them for listening to us endlessly talk about it, for being there when we called late at night or hours before a deadline requesting "quick reads" and feedback, for missing time with friends to re-write and re-think one more paragraph, for talking about cars when they would rather talk about movies, politics, world affairs, or fashion! Our friends turned around on highways to hear us speak so they could witness first hand audience reactions to the book. Coffee klatches turned into cover reviews. Our dealers couldn't get their month end stats tallied because we needed them to read the final draft.

We didn't even give Marti's 83 year old mother a pass when her printer broke down at page 126 and her aunt Sara had to drop everything so she and dad could continue reading. Our efforts have been fortified by so many we can't begin to express the depth of our gratitude.

We had a once in a lifetime opportunity to work with Sunny 95/WSNY 94.7FM (owned by Saga Communications, Inc.), the number one radio station in Columbus, Ohio. Sunny 95/WSNY 94.7FM held a series of focus groups on women automobile buyers that, in part, became the Voice of the Customer chapter. To Alan Goodman, Chris Forgy, Katie Corbin Cyr, and Chuck Knight: your dedication to doing it right is an example to every person, organization, or company striving to serve the women's market.

To Judy Semplinski, John Pockrus and Mike Eagle: thank you for being our eyes and ears into the dealer and sales community and generously sharing your expertise and experiences. Special thanks to Harry Cohen, Devon Cohen, Maureen Kempstone-Darkes, and Alex Florence for reading the book and providing invaluable feedback. This book is as much about your dedication to the automobile industry as it is about your unselfish support of our project.

Many thanks to Dr. Richard Zuliani for teaching us the science of Competency Modeling.

To Jane Brown a deeply felt, "we couldn't have done it without you."

When we had only a concept, Bonnie Smith stepped out and conducted the initial research that convinced us there was a need for this book. Bonnie, you got us off and running. Thank you.

And in the tradition of saving the best until last, to Dan Maddox Jr., for reading every draft quickly and providing invaluable feedback and support. You are one of a kind, and every person should be so lucky to have a big brother like you.

P.S. Let's be clear: We didn't mean to suggest either of us is anywhere near "greatness." But our friends and family are helping us to at least move in the right direction. You make us better. Thank you.

Rebecca Maddox & Marti Smye

MaddoxSmye, LLC, was founded in 1993 with the mission to help companies convert more women shoppers into buyers, long-term customers and vocal advocates. The firm has spent the last ten years studying and developing an understanding of how women think, decide, shop, and buy, as well as how they talk about their experiences, what they value, and what a company must do to win their long-term loyalties. They have developed a unique track record that consistently translates into incremental, measurable sales for a blue chip roster of client companies.

MaddoxSmye, LLC, has delivered training seminars on how to sell cars to women to over 500 car dealerships nationwide. The automotive industry now represents over 60% of the firm's revenues.

The combination of Rebecca Maddox's expertise and knowledge of what women want with Dr. Marti Smye's three decades of hands-on experience and writing in the field of change management, provides companies with an unbeatable road map, showing them the way to tap into this exploding and very profitable market.

Whether the work needed is strategic, tactical, group seminars or one-on-one consultations—MaddoxSmye's focus is to help you sell more of your product to women, whether that product is cars, computers, or annuities.

The Authors

Rebecca Maddox, M.B.A., C.P.A., is a Founding Principal of MaddoxSmye, LLC. In 1990, she was the first business executive to recognize the women's market, as noted by *The Wall Street Journal*. In 1995, she started working in the automotive industry at the dealership level, and she has since worked with virtually every car brand/manufacturer.

Prior to founding MaddoxSmye, LLC, she had a successful 20-year career in Corporate America, during which time she held executive positions as Senior Vice President of Marketing and Sales with Capital Holding (a $33 billion diversified financial services company), Citigroup, and Comp-U-Card of America.

Ms. Maddox has been interviewed about women and how to sell to them by major media sources in the U.S., including: CNBC, CNN, *The Wall Street Journal*, *The New York Times*, and *Business Week*. She is also a much sought after speaker for annual conventions and meetings across the country. Ms. Maddox is a member of the National Speakers Association (NSA) and the best-selling author of *Inc. Your Dreams*.

Since 1994, she has served on the Board of Directors of *Right Management Consultants, Inc.* (NYSE Symbol: RHT), which was ranked #5 on *Forbes* magazines' "List of 200 Best Managed Small Companies" in 2002 and has been on the "List" for five straight years.

Ms. Maddox has an M.B.A. in Marketing and Finance from Columbia University, a B.A. from Pennsylvania State University, and she received her C.P.A. designation from the state of New York in 1975. When she is not traveling to dealerships, she resides in Naples, Florida.

Marti Smye, Ph.D., is a Founding Principal of MaddoxSmye, LLC, and a recognized thought leader in managing change. Her accomplishments include founding the largest change management consulting company in Canada, which consulted with Fortune 500 clients. She was President of the Worldwide Consulting Division of *Right Management Consultants, Inc.*, the world's leading career transition and organizational consulting firm. She currently leads the Coaching and Executive Development Division for *Korn/Ferry International*, the largest executive search firm in the world.

Dr. Smye is an accomplished writer and has written several books on change and career management including *You Don't Change a Company by Memo* and *Is It Too Late to Run Away and Join the Circus?* She has been seen, heard, and read in countless television, radio and print interviews including NBC's *Today* show.

Dr. Smye completed the Harvard Business School's Owners, Presidents, and Managers program and received her M.Ed. and Ph.D. from the University of Toronto.

Denise Ciencin, M.A., has worked with at-risk teenagers, displaced homemakers, the developmentally disabled, and many other populations in crisis. She was listed in the 2001 edition of *Who's Who in America*. She has also written in the fields of neurology and neurosurgery, and she recently sold her first novel. Ms. Ciencin received her M.A. in Community Counseling from Rollins College and she lives in Ft. Myers, FL.

Scott Ciencin is a *New York Times* best-selling author. He has published more than 50 books with Random House, Simon and Schuster, Avon, Kensington, and many more publishers. He began his career writing and directing for television, and he enjoys working in many mediums. His original adventure series *Dinoverse* has been optioned as a feature film, and he numbers Paramount, Universal, and Sony among his clientele. He lives in Ft. Myers, FL, with his beloved wife, Denise.

The Watson Guides™
How to Get
RICH
Selling Cars
to *Women!*

To Order Additional Copies of the Book or
The Watson Guides™ Training Materials
Contact MaddoxSmye, LLC Sales Department at:
(416) 483-3955
Email: rmaddox@maddoxsmye.com
Website: www.maddoxsmye.com
The Watson Guides™: How to Get Rich Selling
Cars to Women 0-9727637-0-8 $27.95 ($38.95 CAN)

ORDER FORM
Payable in US funds only. We accept Visa, MC ($30.00 min.) and
money orders. No Cash/COD. Call (416) 483-3955, fax (416) 483-5085
or e-mail rmaddox@maddoxsmye.com with orders:

Bill my credit card # _____

Visa _____ MC _____ Expiration Date _____

Signature _____

Address _____

City _____ ST _____ ZIP _____

Daytime phone # _____

Ship to _____

Address _____

City _____ ST _____ ZIP _____

# of Copies	Price Per Book
1-15	$27.95
16-49	$23.00
50-500	$20.00
over 500	$15.00
over 2000	$12.00
Book Total	$_____
Sales Tax (if applicable)	$_____
Postage & Handling	$_____
Total Amount Due	$_____

Can/Int'l orders please allow 6-8 weeks.
This offer is subject to change without notice.